BRIDGE
WITH MY
GRANDDAUGHTER

P.F. Saunders

Mr. Bridge

First published 1992 by Mr Bridge Limited
Ryden Grange, Limecroft Road, Bisley, Surrey

Distributed by Milestone Publications
62 Murray Road, Horndean, Hampshire

Series Editor: Elena Jeronimidis
Technical Consultant: Eric Crowhurst
Front Cover: Brian Best

Typeset by Ruth Edmondson, Calstock, Cornwall
Printed in Great Britain by Ashford Colour Press, Gosport, Hampshire

ISBN 1 85265 123 7

CONTENTS

To my daughter, Diana

FOREWORD

When BRIDGE PLUS was half-way through its second year, I received a polite letter in which a ninety-year-old gentleman hesitantly submitted an article for publication. It took me some time to come to grips with the fact that this was no other than the famous P.F. Saunders, creator of the immortal 'Wilson' and author of *Bridge With My Wife*. The article was vintage Saunders and, as soon as I recovered from my astonished delight, I contacted the author with a view to establishing whether he would be willing to write a few more articles for our magazine.

Yes, Mr Saunders had a few more stories about the bridge-playing young woman and her grandfather, and he would be happy to send them on. What he did not say at the time was that his little cache amounted to thirty-odd articles, and when I discovered this – through other, even more hesitant letters – the fate of *Bridge With My Granddaughter* was sealed. BRIDGE PLUS, a monthly magazine, would take years to publish all those lovely stories – a book was needed to bring them all together to the attention and the enjoyment of our readers and other bridge players.

Once more, I contacted P.F. Saunders to ask what he thought of this project. This time, there was no hesitation – and the author's enthusiasm found an echo in the publisher, who set about the production of the book in record time. My only worry, as Editor of BRIDGE PLUS, was that I might no longer have a fresh supply of original Saunders' articles for the magazine. But no – in his usual quiet, unassuming way the author assured me that he would carry on writing. That's a promise, P.F., and now all your readers are holding you to it!

Elena Jeronimidis

THE TRUTH

"Would you like to hear about some bridge-table brilliance?" my granddaughter asked me.

"Very much. Especially if it concerns you."

"Oh, it concerns me all right. I was roped in to play in last night's pairs and partner a man I'd never met, obviously a rather good player. I was West, dealer on this board, and I opened with a bid of three clubs. All right so far?"

West	North	East	South
3♣	NB	NB	4♠

Game All; Dealer West

```
                ♠ 8
                ♥ J 10 5 3
                ♦ A Q 9 6 5 2
                ♣ 8 5
♠ A 6 5                      ♠ 9 7 3
♥ 6            N            ♥ Q 9 7 2
♦ 10 3       W   E          ♦ J 8 7 4
♣ K Q J 9 7 4 2   S         ♣ A 3
                ♠ K Q J 10 4 2
                ♥ A K 8 4
                ♦ K
                ♣ 10 6
```

"Fair enough with a strange partner. I'd have bid one club."

"That's interesting, as you'll see. South jumped to four spades and I led the King of clubs. My partner overtook and returned a club to my Jack. What would you have led next?"

"A diamond, I suppose."

"Well, I preferred to lead the Queen of clubs – no, no comment just yet, please. Declarer ruffed with dummy's eight of spades, my partner covered with the nine, and declarer with the Ten. Now the King of trumps came to my Ace, and I was on lead again. Another club seemed obvious this time, and, to my surprise, my partner ruffed again with the seven of spades, drawing South's Jack. I was getting bemused, and before long I was staggered, though I hope I didn't show it, when my five of spades fell to the Queen, and my six became the highest trump and downed the contract."

"Splendid. But *why* did you decide to lead a third club at the third trick, giving South a ruff and perhaps a valuable discard?"

"Ah, here's where I have to confess to two reasons for feeling rather ashamed. My dear partner asked me the same question. I had pulled myself rapidly together by then and sweetly replied 'It seemed a good idea at the time.' He looked hard at me, but did not press the matter."

"The truth being . . .?"

"Haven't you guessed? I had miscounted clubs! I think I must have given myself only six, because I felt sure that South had another. I thought that my partner might be able to win over dummy's ruff. It turned out that we were the only pair to get the four spade contract down, and I had been responsible by giving my partner the chance to apply a double upper-cut!"

"Was every South in four spades?"

"Some were in three only – probably, my partner thought, because West opened with one club, in some ways a more off-putting bid than a pre-empt. So that's one up to you. But I ought to have told the truth at the time. Grandfathers have their uses. You don't mind being a sort of confessional?"

"Any time."

GUESSING RIGHT

"This time I'm bringing you something really important," my grand-daughter told me. "A hand from last night's rubber bridge, when Bruce and I had a catastrophe. We could have made three no-trumps with an overtrick, or five clubs easily, and actually went one down in four hearts. You've got to say whose fault it was. Don't look at the East-West hands more than you can help. It's our North-South bidding I want you to concentrate on. I was South."

South	West	North	East
1♥	3♦	Dbl	NB
3♠	NB	4♥	End

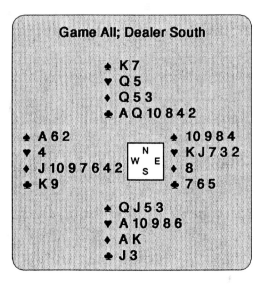

Game All; Dealer South

```
            ♠ K 7
            ♥ Q 5
            ♦ Q 5 3
            ♣ A Q 10 8 4 2
♠ A 6 2                    ♠ 10 9 8 4
♥ 4            N           ♥ K J 7 3 2
♦ J 10 9 7 6 4 2  W  E     ♦ 8
♣ K 9            S         ♣ 7 6 5
            ♠ Q J 5 3
            ♥ A 10 9 8 6
            ♦ A K
            ♣ J 3
```

"Well, I can see that West's cheeky jump bid put your partner in a slight difficulty. I'd have made the natural call of four clubs, but I expect he didn't want to rule out three no-trumps, which might be the best contract. What did his double mean?"

"I thought it was negative, not a business double, espe-cially in view of my top diamonds, showing a useful hand with no obvious bid. I was strong enough, I thought, to reverse into three spades."

"So he knew nothing about your diamonds, and you knew nothing about his clubs. I think three no-trumps would have been better."

"Anyway he put me with long, strong hearts, and there we were in a heart game."

"*He* might have tried three no-trumps at that point instead of four hearts. By the way, did you think of leaving his double in? It looks as if that would have made your fortune. As it was, how did the play go?"

"West led the Jack of diamonds to my Ace, and I played a heart to dummy's Queen and East's King. East then led a spade to his partner's Ace, and ruffed the diamond return, so I had lost three of the first four tricks and had to make the rest. Another spade from East put me in dummy, and I brought off a heart finesse only to find that West had no more. I successfully ran the Jack of clubs and then dropped the King, leaving myself in dummy with nothing but winners – but with East still holding Jack-seven of hearts and myself holding the Ace-Ten-nine and two useless spade winners. East, of course, refused to ruff dummy's diamond and clubs, so I found myself furiously ruffing my own winners at the eleventh trick and surrendering to his Jack of trumps at the thirteenth."

"Couldn't you have shortened your trumps to match his? At the fifth trick why not ruff your good Queen of diamonds, so that you have three trumps over his three? Then you take your club finesse, followed by the heart finesse and another club to the Ace, and finally turn your attention to the club suit. At the end you have the Ace-Ten over East's Jack -seven."

"I never thought of it! So, all it amounts to is that my partner's double was wrong, my spade bid was wrong, his heart bid was wrong, the contract was wrong, and my playing of the wrong contract was very wrong. I shall have to be very careful how I pass this on to Bruce. As I told you at the beginning, it's very important, because . . . because . . ." For once my granddaughter was at a loss for words.

I still have moments of inspiration. "Is it" I asked (and I knew almost at once that I was right) "because partners need to understand each other's bidding before deciding to become life partners?"

THAT'S DIFFERENT

"Here's another bidding question for you," my granddaughter told me. "East on my right opens with one spade, and I hold:

♠A 10 4 2   ♥Q 10 3 2   ♦10 8 5   ♣A K

"Do I bid one no-trump? Or double? Or make a trap pass? This is rubber bridge, a women's four. At the golf club," she added rather apologetically.

"I like the first bid. The second might be misleading. I hate the third."

"Then for once I got it right. My partner raised me to two no-trumps, East bid three hearts, and I doubled. North hesitated, then put me into three no-trumps. This was the hand."

East	South	West	North
1♠	1NT	NB	2NT
3♥	Dbl	NB	3NT

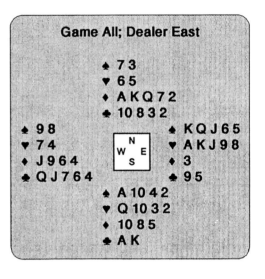

Game All; Dealer East

	♠ 7 3	
	♥ 6 5	
	♦ A K Q 7 2	
	♣ 10 8 3 2	
♠ 9 8		♠ K Q J 6 5
♥ 7 4		♥ A K J 9 8
♦ J 9 6 4		♦ 3
♣ Q J 7 6 4		♣ 9 5
	♠ A 10 4 2	
	♥ Q 10 3 2	
	♦ 10 8 5	
	♣ A K	

"Tell me," I said, after examining the diagram. "How good a golfer is your partner?"

"Five handicap, I think. What's that got to do with it?"

"Ah, I thought that golf might really be her game. Oughtn't she to have gone straight to three no-trumps? It's not all that often one can provide five probable tricks! And surely she committed a rubber bridge crime in not trusting your double?"

"Yes, I think we could have got them three down."

"And remained as likely to win the rubber as before."

"You said she ought to have gone straight to three no-trumps. Are you telling me I ought to have made it?"

"Are you telling me you didn't?"

"West led the nine of spades, and I could see that if the diamonds behaved, I had eight tricks on top. I won with the Ace and led the five of diamonds, but East showed out on the second round, so I switched to a heart. East won, played the King and Queen of spades, and threw me in with another spade to my Ten. I crossed with a third diamond to lead another heart, but East won and put me down with her last spade. So much for your five tricks in dummy, there turned out to be only three!"

"Couldn't you have played the diamonds differently? Look at that seven in dummy."

"What's so special about the seven?"

"It's the same as your eight . . . No, I'm not being silly. You know from East's cheerful bidding that she held at least ten major-suit cards. Instead of hoping that the diamonds 'behaved', why not put West with four of them and lead the *eight*, not the five, at trick two? You overtake with the Queen, return to hand with a club, and lead the Ten of diamonds, running it if West does not cover. If West covers, you win, return with another club, and can see the Ace-seven of diamonds tenace in dummy, over West's nine-six, through which you lead your *five*."

"How clever of me. So I make five diamonds. That's only eight tricks!"

"Yes. But you know what East holds. Look at the five card ending. Lead either a spade or a heart from dummy, and East has to give you a second spade winner and your contract."

"One more question. Why, when you're playing with me, do you insist on my having at least fifteen points for a no-trump overcall?"

"Because you have a male partner."

"I *knew* you would make a sexist comment before long!"

```
                ♠ 7
                ♥ 6 5
                ♦ —
                ♣ 10 8
 ♠ 8                        ♠ K Q 6
 ♥ 7 4      N               ♥ A K
 ♦ —    W       E           ♦ —
 ♣ Q J      S               ♣ —
                ♠ 10 4 2
                ♥ Q 10
                ♦ —
                ♣ —
```

PROVING A POINT

"Now we shall see," said my granddaughter, as she cut with her boyfriend, Bruce, to play against their elders and betters. It was our near-family Rubber Bridge Four, the other pair being myself and my regular club partner, known to one and all as 'Paddy' (but he is not an Irishman), and incidentally the best player of the four.

"What shall we see?" I asked.

"Do you know," she went on, addressing no-one in particular, "that yesterday I was called pig-headed by my own grandfather?"

"Untrue," I protested, as I began to deal. "The word I used was 'intransigent', and I applied it to both of us in certain bridge matters."

"Well, you meant me," she said, as she sorted her hand.

"Anyhow," I said, "I'm opening with four hearts."

There were two passes. "And I," she retorted, "am bidding an intransigent five diamonds." Everybody passed.

I led the Ace of hearts, then the King which declarer ruffed. She drew trumps, played three winning clubs ending in dummy, ruffed a third round of hearts, and ended by losing two spades and the contract. There was silence while we entered the score.

West	North	East	South
4♥	NB	NB	5♦

Love All; Dealer West

```
              ♠ A 6 5 2
              ♥ 9 4 3
              ♦ 7 5 3
              ♣ Q 10 6
♠ —                        ♠ K Q J 10 8 4
♥ A K Q J 10 7 2    N      ♥ 8 6
♦ J 4            W     E    ♦ 10 9
♣ J 9 5 3            S      ♣ 8 4 2
              ♠ 9 7 3
              ♥ 5
              ♦ A K Q 8 6 2
              ♣ A K 7
```

"I've a sort of feeling," she said, "that somebody is being rather kind. One of my opponents has his quizzical expression, and the other looks as if he's biting his tongue."

"I was wondering," I admitted, "what was in your mind on that hand."

"Not a lot. I had ten tricks on top, but dummy was so *flat* . . ."

"Now who's being personal?" interrupted Bruce.

". . . that I was bound to lose a heart and two spades."

"But what did dummy's cards look like after you had drawn trumps and played three clubs?"

"Much the same, but fewer."

"I mean what had you gained by eliminating clubs?"

"Three tricks."

"Oh, come *on*," said her partner. "You now had a void in both hands."

"*And* an almost complete count of the hand," put in Paddy. "You knew that my partner had started with seven hearts, two diamonds and now three clubs, together with either the last club or a singleton spade. Instead of leading dummy's last heart for a ruff, play the Ace of spades to remove West's singleton (if he has one), then the heart – not for a ruff, but for the discard of a losing spade. West is thrown in and has to lead either the Jack of clubs or another heart."

"Yes," I added, "then dummy's much despised third trump takes the trick, while you throw the last of your spades."

"I wasn't so 'flat' after all," pointed out Bruce.

"What it all comes to, I suppose," I said, as I cut to him for the second deal, "is that the lucky trump break and then the possibility of counting the hand threw a different light on the whole thing. You had to start reconsidering everything."

There was another silence, while we sorted our new cards, until Paddy broke it. There was a twinkle in his eye as he said, "In other words . . ."

My granddaughter stopped frowning and looked at him. "Oh, I see," she said slowly. "You all think I was being . . . whatever it was that he said that I was." She was as amused as the rest of us. "Well," she concluded, "at least I was right about one thing. I said we'd see – and we did!"

TWO OF A KIND

"When and where did you first meet Paddy?" asked my granddaughter.

"At the bridge table, of course, nearly thirty years ago. We had cut against each other at a rubber bridge club in Eastbourne, where we were both on holiday. Two momentous hands, which we have never forgotten, really brought us together."

"*Please* tell me about them."

"I'll write them down for you. This was the first, which came early on. Paddy was South, and I was West. I led the King of diamonds against his four hearts, and I

East	South	West	North
3♦	3♥	NB	3NT
NB	4♥	End	

remember waiting for him to play dummy's Ace and thinking that he looked a good chap but was probably a beginner. At last he played the *three*, not the Ace, and I had to lead again. I was just going to lead my other diamond, when I suddenly thought that, in view of my partner's call, Paddy probably had a singleton. So perhaps he wanted to discard something on the second round of

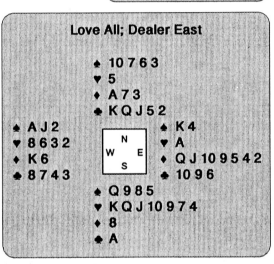

Love All; Dealer East

```
              ♠ 10 7 6 3
              ♥ 5
              ♦ A 7 3
              ♣ K Q J 5 2
♠ A J 2                      ♠ K 4
♥ 8 6 3 2         N          ♥ A
♦ K 6         W     E        ♦ Q J 10 9 5 4 2
♣ 8 7 4 3         S          ♣ 10 9 6
              ♠ Q 9 8 5
              ♥ K Q J 10 9 7 4
              ♦ 8
              ♣ A
```

diamonds? I therefore switched to a trump, which went to East's Ace. Now it was my partner's turn to be fogged. After a long pause he shrugged and led another diamond. You can see what happened. Paddy discarded his Ace of clubs on the Ace of diamonds, threw three losing spades on dummy's clubs and made his contract. If East had led anything but a diamond, he would have gone down. Paddy knew that I had been let down and gave me a sympathetic glance. I'm not sure he didn't give me a wink!"

"How sweet. I wish I'd been there."

"Then later in the evening came a curiously similar hand. Paddy was once more declarer in a four heart contract, against which I led the six of spades, my partner's suit.

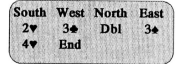

South	West	North	East
2♥	3♣	Dbl	3♠
4♥	End		

"Paddy won and led the King of hearts to my Ace, and I put East in with a second spade. Declarer ruffed a third round of spades with the Ten, and I was about to overruff with my Jack, when two thoughts suddenly came to me. First that by ruffing I would establish dummy's nine of trumps as an entry; second, that either East or South must be void of clubs. Perhaps South was void and was locked out of dummy? Instead of ruffing, I discarded a club! Paddy removed my trump, but he had already lost two tricks and now had to lose two diamonds. He was most appreciative of my defence afterwards, and we found ourselves enjoying each other's company and exchanging telephone numbers, and we've been life-long bridge partners ever since."

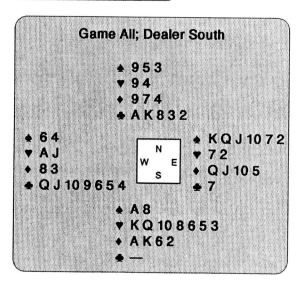

Game All; Dealer South

♠ 9 5 3
♥ 9 4
♦ 9 7 4
♣ A K 8 3 2

♠ 6 4
♥ A J
♦ 8 3
♣ Q J 10 9 6 5 4

♠ K Q J 10 7 2
♥ 7 2
♦ Q J 10 5
♣ 7

♠ A 8
♥ K Q 10 8 6 5 3
♦ A K 6 2
♣ —

"It's a wonderful story."

"There's a post-script to it. In the middle of that same night my bed-side telephone rang. 'That hand when you refused to overruff,' I heard. 'I could have made it. I play two rounds of diamonds, throw you in with a trump to your Jack, and make you lead a club. Good-night'."

"I've often wondered who was the craftier of you two. I'm still not sure!"

IN DISGRACE

"I'm in disgrace with Paddy," I told my granddaughter and young Bruce.

"I'm not letting anyone bully you, not even Paddy," declared my granddaughter.

"I failed him twice last night in the match, and as a penance I promised him I'd show you the two boards. In both of them I was East, defending against game contracts, and you two have to guess what happened. This was the first," I said, scribbling the hand below.

North	South
1♦	1NT
2NT	3♣
3NT	End

Love All; Dealer North

```
              ♠ A K 5
              ♥ A Q 6
              ♦ A 8 3 2
              ♣ 8 5 3
   ♠ Q 9 3            N        ♠ 10 8 4 2
   ♥ K 7 3        W       E    ♥ J 10 8 5 2
   ♦ K Q J 10 4       S        ♦ 9 5
   ♣ Q 7                       ♣ K 4
              ♠ J 7 6
              ♥ 9 4
              ♦ 7 6
              ♣ A J 10 9 6 2
```

"Paddy, who was West, led the King of diamonds, which was ducked, then the Queen. South won and led a small club from dummy. Over to you."

"Well," said Bruce after a little thought, "I think you've more or less told us yourself what happened. I'm guessing that you played the four of clubs like any sane person, and that you ought to have gone up with the King. But why should you?"

"Because a glance at dummy should have told me that there was only one chance of Paddy getting in and playing off his diamond winners – he just might hold the Queen of clubs, and, if he did, it would probably be a doubleton because of South's bidding. You're right. I played low, South went up with the Ace, Paddy never got in, and South made an overtrick."

"But if you go up with the King, South can duck, and cash the Ace of clubs next, can't he?" asked Bruce hesitantly. "Then West is still kept off lead."

"Yes, and anyway, I don't like South," commented my granddaughter, "or his no-trump bid. It's that stupid business of not being allowed to call clubs with only six points. He was very lucky. Show us the other hand."

I produced this deal.

West	North	East	South
1♥	NB	2♥	3♦
4♥	5♦	End	

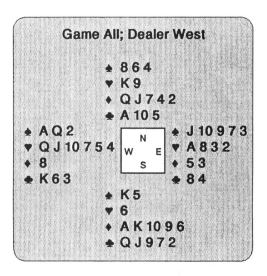

Game All; Dealer West

```
              ♠ 8 6 4
              ♥ K 9
              ♦ Q J 7 4 2
              ♣ A 10 5
♠ A Q 2              ┌─────┐   ♠ J 10 9 7 3
♥ Q J 10 7 5 4      │  N  │   ♥ A 8 3 2
♦ 8                 │W   E│   ♦ 5 3
♣ K 6 3             │  S  │   ♣ 8 4
                    └─────┘
              ♠ K 5
              ♥ 6
              ♦ A K 10 9 6
              ♣ Q J 9 7 2
```

"This time Paddy led the Queen of hearts against the contract, and after a moment's thought South played dummy's nine."

"Yes, go on."

"No – here's where *you* go on."

"Oh, I see. Well, East encourages with the eight, of course."

"Doesn't he stop to consider why South didn't cover?"

"He didn't cover," suggested Bruce, "in case East had a singleton Ace."

"West therefore having nine in the suit? No, he had a better reason than that. He simply wanted the lead to remain on his left. He probably thought that the elderly, complacent gentleman on his right might be persuaded not to play his Ace over his partner's winners and lead a spade to defeat the contract in the first three tricks! He was right, and so were you – I played the eight. South ruffed the heart continuation, drew trumps, ran off five clubs with the help of a finesse, and discarded two of dummy's spades. He could now ruff a spade at the end and lose only one heart and one spade. It only remains to be said that in the other room the same two contracts were both defeated."

"And I suppose," said my granddaughter, "that Paddy quite enjoyed telling you what you might have done. I hope you replied that you could remember the old days when Bridge was a good, clean game."

"Yes," added Bruce, "and that it was all his fault for taking you off to play in this Teams match instead of coming to play rubber bridge with the three of us here."

"Where we do *not* overtake our partner's winners."

"And where second hand invariably plays *low*."

"And where *nobody*," concluded my granddaughter, "is ever in disgrace with anybody."

"Thanks," I said. "I'll pass all that on. I'm feeling better!"

CHRISTMAS BRIDGE

My granddaughter had never before spent Christmas away from her parents, but this year my daughter and son-in-law were in America, so the two of us were on our own. This was Christmas Eve, and we had been promised a telephone call across the Atlantic on Christmas Day.

The local bridge club had been enterprising in organising a Christmas Eve Pairs competition, in which all four members of our recently formed Rubber Bridge Regular Four – two ancients, Paddy and myself, and two youngsters, Bruce and my granddaughter – had taken part. It had been a cheerful, draw-for-partners affair, with strange variations of the rules of bridge being suddenly introduced at chosen moments, to cause hilarity in the young-at-heart but confusion in the traditionalists. Bruce, for example, who takes certain aspects of life seriously (bridge among them) was, I could see, nobly pretending to enjoy himself, and I suppose that the same applies to me. Paddy and my granddaughter, however, had no such inhibitions and could generally be found at one or other of the noisier tables. We had agreed beforehand that we would meet again later in the day for a quiet supper and a rubber or two of real bridge before going to bed at a reasonable hour and preparing ourselves for tomorrow.

One hand that we played that evening was worth recording. Here it is. It was the last deal of the short session before bed-time.

South	West	North	East
1♣	Dbl	3♣	NB
5♣	Dbl	End	

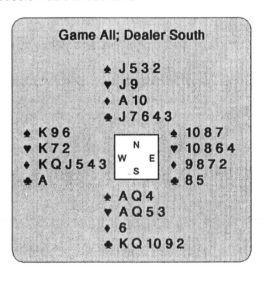

Game All; Dealer South

```
                ♠ J 5 3 2
                ♥ J 9
                ♦ A 10
                ♣ J 7 6 4 3
♠ K 9 6                      ♠ 10 8 7
♥ K 7 2          N           ♥ 10 8 6 4
♦ K Q J 5 4 3  W   E         ♦ 9 8 7 2
♣ A              S           ♣ 8 5
                ♠ A Q 4
                ♥ A Q 5 3
                ♦ 6
                ♣ K Q 10 9 2
```

There was just a trace of Christmas spirit in the auction. My granddaughter dealt and opened one club. I was West and doubled, and Bruce raised his partner to three – a pre-emptive bid which might have meant a weaker hand. South was not deterred, however, from jumping to game, and I made a light-hearted double.

I then led the King of diamonds, won by dummy's Ace. After a little thought South played the Ten of diamonds, which she ruffed, and then a club to my singleton Ace. I was endplayed at trick three! My discomfort became obvious, as also did my partner Paddy's amusement. At last, I decided to lead the six of spades. South won with the Queen, drew the remaining trump, and played the Ace and a third spade, and I was in again! What's more, the thirteenth spade was established in dummy. By this time both my opponents had begun to see the funny side of it. I still refused to lead a diamond and allow a ruff and discard, so tried the two of hearts, only to see dummy's Jack win and declarer claim her contract.

Paddy broke the silence. "There was a time," he said, "when grandparents were treated with a little respect. I've never seen one so neatly tied into knots."

"You don't mind, do you?" said the almost contrite declarer to me. "It's all your doing really. You told me the other day that I must *not* go on *automatically* leading trumps at the first opportunity. I remembered just in time and ruffed that diamond instead. I hoped it might make things awkward for you."

"It certainly did. Well done!"

"What's more," went on Paddy, "she found the only way to make the contract. There was not a thing you could do about it from start to finish."

"Suppose," said Bruce unexpectedly, "that West's opening lead is the Ace of trumps?"

Paddy and I looked at one another.

"Do you know," he said, "I believe he's right and I'm wrong? Then you could be thrown in only once, and are bound to make both Kings. It's time you stopped making these 'automatic' opening leads."

I'm not sure who was the most delighted by the whole thing, the declarer herself, her admiring partner, or her venerable opponents – who had been put in their place for the first time ever!

HARD TO TELL

I am not nearly as good a bridge player as my granddaughter seems to think, but I am human enough to like being regarded as an expert, and I try to keep it that way. She sometimes brings problems to me, especially after playing with young Bruce in the local Pairs, when she has gone down in contracts made by others. This was an example.

North	South
1NT	3♠
4♣	5♣
5♦	6♠

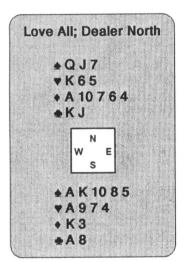

Love All; Dealer North

♠ Q J 7
♥ K 6 5
♦ A 10 7 6 4
♣ K J

♠ A K 10 8 5
♥ A 9 7 4
♦ K 3
♣ A 8

"Here are our cards and the auction," she told me. "West led the Jack of diamonds. Would you like me to tell you first what went on in my mind?"

"Yes, then we can compare it with what goes on in mine."

"As there were eleven tricks on top, I decided that the twelfth must come from a third diamond or a third heart."

"Yes, I'm with you so far."

"I won the diamond lead with my King, didn't like the look of that opening Jack, so drew trumps and started by ducking a heart . . ."

"Stop. I want to think. I've got a feeling that's not right. It's that opening lead that worries me. When you mentioned it and I saw the Ten in dummy, I wondered what West was at. He must have led a singleton Jack – an odd opening lead, though not quite a blind one since North had cue-bid the Ace. Can you think of any diamond holding other than a singleton, from which anyone not holding the Ten would open with the Jack? Of course West might be one of those jokers pretending not to hold the Queen, but I would regard the singleton as a practical certainty."

"And do what about it?"

"Before you tell me what you did do, do you mind writing something with that pencil? Just write 'North ♦ A 10 7 – East ♦ Q 9 8'."

"What's all that about?"

"Suppose that West's Jack is a singleton (It was? Good!) and that East holds five. And suppose that you start by playing out all your winners except Dummy's Ace of diamonds, you reach that end position you've just written down. Now you lead your small diamond to dummy's seven and win the last two tricks and the contract."

"You've solved the whole thing without playing a trick? It's incredible! I'm not sure I like having a wizard for a grandfather!"

"I'm afraid it's not as simple as that. East may not be quite so obliging. So let's look at the whole hand."

"All I could do was make the eleven quick tricks."

"Suppose that after drawing trumps you start playing winners. East will have to find six discards. He need not keep more than two diamonds, so he would end up with the Queen-nine of diamonds and the Ten of clubs, which would spoil our nice little end position. Give me that pencil. Let's try a four-card end position.

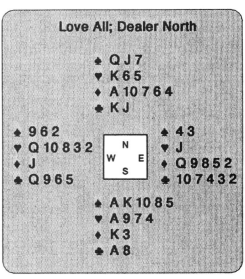

Love All; Dealer North

♠ Q J 7
♥ K 6 5
♦ A 10 7 6 4
♣ K J

♠ 9 6 2
♥ Q 10 8 3 2
♦ J
♣ Q 9 6 5

♠ 4 3
♥ J
♦ Q 9 8 5 2
♣ 10 7 4 3 2

♠ A K 10 8 5
♥ A 9 7 4
♦ K 3
♣ A 8

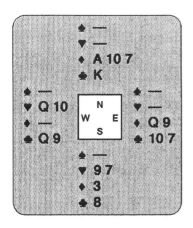

♠ —
♥ —
♦ A 10 7
♣ K

♥ Q 10
♣ Q 9

♦ Q 9
♣ 10 7

♠ —
♥ 9 7
♦ 3
♣ 8

"Suppose you play all your winners *except* dummy's Ace of diamonds *and* King of Clubs. Look. Once more all you have to do is play your diamond to the seven and you make the contract. It doesn't matter what he discards on your winners, you'll know what he holds and can endplay him."

I must admit that I sighed with relief when all went well. I'm not sure I didn't mop my brow. Anyhow, we were both delighted with the way it had worked out and found ourselves laughing out loud.

I wish I was always as successful with her problems. I look forward to them and to our exchanging ideas. Above all I enjoy humouring her. Or is it sometimes she who is doing the humouring?

TAKE YOUR CHOICE

I was West and after two passes I opened the bidding with three hearts, which young Bruce on my left doubled.

"Are you still playing 'optional' doubles of opening threes?" asked my partner, Paddy.

"Yes, in a way." said my granddaughter.

"What's that mean?"

"It's rather difficult to explain."

"What she means," said Bruce, coming to his partner's rescue "is that we play 'optionals', but actually she always takes out my doubles of threes, and I always leave hers in."

"I see. Well, in that case I say 'No Bid'."

"Five diamonds." said my granddaughter.

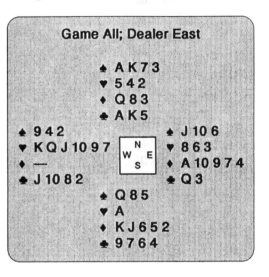

East	South	West	North
NB	NB	3♥	Dbl
NB	5♦	End	

I led the King of hearts, and the play was soon over. South won with the Ace, led a diamond, threatened to tell me exactly what she thought of me and my void, lost to Paddy's Ace, was forced to ruff another heart and ended by losing three trumps and one club. Two down.

Game All; Dealer East

```
                 ♠ A K 7 3
                 ♥ 5 4 2
                 ♦ Q 8 3
                 ♣ A K 5
    ♠ 9 4 2                    ♠ J 10 6
    ♥ K Q J 10 9 7    N        ♥ 8 6 3
    ♦ —            W   E       ♦ A 10 9 7 4
    ♣ J 10 8 2        S        ♣ Q 3
                 ♠ Q 8 5
                 ♥ A
                 ♦ K J 6 5 2
                 ♣ 9 7 6 4
```

"I wonder," she said slowly, "why Paddy didn't double. It was very sweet of him, but we don't ever want favours, do we, Bruce?"

"No," said Bruce "that was understood from the beginning."

"If I had doubled," said Paddy, "*that* would have been doing you a favour. Let's look at the hand again later."

At the end of the rubber we set the cards out, and the first thing to come under criticism was my opening bid.

"A little off-beat, I admit," I said, "but opening threes must not become stereotyped."

"Exactly," said my partner, "and that's one of the reasons for my not doubling your contract, but the main thing is that I would have told you how to play the hand. If I had doubled, you would have been almost sure that I had all the trumps. The opening bid told you that there were shortages about, and a double would have told you where."

"What would I do about it?"

"*Not* lead trumps from your own hand. Cross to dummy first and lead from there. You win with the Jack, see that drawing trumps has no future, start cashing your black suit winners and ruffing dummy's two remaining hearts, and find that you have won the first nine tricks and that the lead is in dummy. Look. You now play the thirteenth spade, overruff East (it would not pay him to go up with the Ace, lead a club and see East having to ruff his partner's club winner and allow dummy's Queen of trumps to become your eleventh winner, giving you the contract and the rubber."

"There you are," she told Bruce. "I was right to take you out of your 'optional'. *You* would have left it in."

"And got them down 500. *And* gone on to win the next game as well."

"I'm beginning to like your system," I told them. "It seems to work whatever you do!"

```
                      ♠ 7
                      ♥ —
                      ♦ Q 8
                      ♣ 5
          ♠ —                      ♠ —
          ♥ Q J      ┌─────┐       ♥ —
          ♦ —        │  N  │       ♦ A 10 9 7
          ♣ J 10     │W   E│       ♣ —
                     │  S  │
                     └─────┘
                      ♠ —
                      ♥ —
                      ♦ J 6
                      ♣ 9 7
```

ROUTINE PLAY

Before I went off to partner Paddy in a Teams semi-final, I rather rashly promised my granddaughter that I would record any deal in which I could take personal pride. I was not to pretend that no such deal had occurred, nor was I to report one where the credit was really Paddy's and not mine. We lost the match, but for once I was responsible for one of the few swings in our favour.

"Suppose," I told her the following day, "that you are South, declarer in a contract of four spades doubled, and that West leads the nine of hearts. This was the auction and these are your cards. What are your prospects?"

East	South	West	North
1♥	1♠	NB	NB
2♦	2♠	NB	4♠
NB	NB	Dbl	End

N/S Vul; Dealer East

♠ 7 6 4
♥ 6 3 2
♦ J 8 7 4
♣ A K 9

```
      N
   W     E
      S
```

♠ K J 10 9 3 2
♥ A Q
♦ K
♣ Q 10 5 3

"East has bid two suits, and West has doubled. I suppose West has Ace and Queen of trumps, but I can't see why I shouldn't lose only two spades and one diamond."

"That's how I saw it, except that I went a bit further and put West with all four missing trumps, partly because he had doubled without, apparently, anything else in his hand, partly because East, with only eleven points seemed likely to have a void to justify his confident re-opening of the auction. Anyway, how would you start?"

"By crossing to dummy with a club and leading a small trump from there."

"I very nearly did just that, but I couldn't get West's probable Ace-Queen-eight-five of spades out of my mind, and I started wondering whether he might not make *three* trump tricks."

"But surely my top four, King-Jack-Ten-nine, can see that lot off?"

"Let's look at the whole hand now."

"I won the opening nine of hearts lead with the Queen. If I go on as you suggested, by crossing to dummy and leading a trump, West wins with the Queen over my nine, leads his second heart, regains the lead with the Ace of trumps over my Ten, and puts East in with a diamond to his Ace. Now East can lead a third heart and promote West's eight of trumps. This is exactly what our East did in the other room and the other South went one down."

"Did you actually foresee that?"

"I did."

```
                    N/S Vul; Dealer East
                    ♠ 7 6 4
                    ♥ 6 3 2
                    ♦ J 8 7 4
                    ♣ A K 9
     ♠ A Q 8 5                      ♠ —
     ♥ 9 4          N               ♥ K J 10 8 7 5
     ♦ 5 3 2     W     E            ♦ A Q 10 9 6
     ♣ 8 6 4 2      S               ♣ J 7
                    ♠ K J 10 9 3 2
                    ♥ A Q
                    ♦ K
                    ♣ Q 10 5 3
```

"And I suppose you're going to tell me what seems even more incredible – that you found something you could do about it?"

"I found a lead for the second trick."

"I shall be hearing next that you led the King of diamonds!"

"You've said it. No promotion of West's eight of trumps could take place if East could be kept out of the lead, and it was easy to see that his only entry card was the Ace of Diamonds. By removing it before the second round of hearts could be led, I cut their communications and lost only two trumps and one diamond."

"Wonderful. West must have kicked himself for doubling."

"And East for not passing one spade."

"Paddy must have been delighted."

"I think he was – later. At the time he simply said 'Flat board'."

"Why? I don't understand."

"To him the King of diamonds was so obvious that he thought any South would play it and make the contract!"

"I shall tell him just what I think of him!"

TIMING TROUBLE

My granddaughter was indignant. "I still don't believe it," she said. We were returning from a club pairs competition, which we had come close to winning, and were remembering one bad board that had brought us down. "I had four certain tricks," she went on. "I shan't sleep unless you explain what happened."

North	East	South	West
NB	NB	1♠	Dbl
3♠	NB	4♠	Dbl
End			

Game All; Dealer North

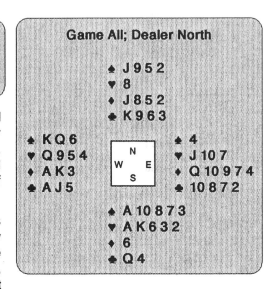

♠ J 9 5 2
♥ 8
♦ J 8 5 2
♣ K 9 6 3

♠ K Q 6
♥ Q 9 5 4
♦ A K 3
♣ A J 5

♠ 4
♥ J 10 7
♦ Q 10 9 7 4
♣ 10 8 7 2

♠ A 10 8 7 3
♥ A K 6 3 2
♦ 6
♣ Q 4

We reconstructed the deal to our satisfaction, then my partner began again, "Yes, that's near enough. I had nineteen points, so of course I doubled him."

"I led the Ace of diamonds and knew, when I saw dummy, that unless there was a void somewhere, and so long as I was not fool enough to lead spades, I must make at least four tricks. You gave me nothing of course . . ."

"Why 'of course'?"

". . . but I didn't expect or need it."

"I believe South knew what he was doing. He could tell from the bidding that you held those winners. He ruffed your diamond continuation at the second trick and led a club, didn't he, which you rightly ducked."

"Yes, then came three rounds of hearts, dummy ruffing the third, then another club to my Ace. Then he ruffed my club return, ruffed another heart with dummy's nine of trumps, and then ruffed another diamond."

"Let's see how that left him, with the lead in his own hand."

"That's it. Now he led his last heart, and you had to ruff with the Queen, while he threw dummy's club. So you had to give him the last two tricks. He was the only South to make four spades. I'm just beginning to wonder . . ."

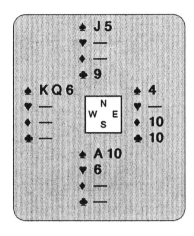

♠ J 5
♥ —
♦ —
♣ 9

♠ K Q 6   ♠ 4
♥ —   ♥ —
♦ —   ♦ 10
♣ —   ♣ 10

          ♠ A 10
          ♥ 6
          ♦ —
          ♣ —

"I don't like the sound of this."

". . . whether you might have switched at the second trick. If you try leading the King of trumps . . ."

"Oh *no!*"

". . . and he wins and leads a club, you go up with the Ace and have the pleasure of leading trumps *twice* more, losing a second of course, but disrupting all that cross-ruffing, which you could guess he was planning. If he wins the spade lead and goes at once for the cross-ruff, he can ruff three diamonds in hand, but then will find himself outnumbered in trumps and losing to your six as well as to your Queen!"

"Suppose he ducks my spade lead at trick two."

"You simply exit with another diamond. You can be quite sure now that your Queen of trumps will be a winner in the end."

"I still think that that endplay was out of this world."

"We were very unlucky to run up against that particular South."

"And to think that a moment ago I said that I was not fool enough to lead a spade!"

"A small timing error. Try saying it again, this time putting 'not' just two words later."

NO HURRY

My granddaughter and I were putting away the cards, after the other two had gone, when she said, "Do you remember that diamond slam, which you made in your typical style?"

"Yes, but what's my 'typical' style?"

"Cool and rather canny."

"I see. Well, let's remember the hand."

"Yes," she went on. "I was West and had to make the opening lead against your six diamonds after a typical auction."

South	North
NB	2NT
3♦	4♦
4♠	5♣
5♦	5♥
6♦	End

"Oh, so my bidding's 'typical' too? Same two adjectives?"

"Let's add a third – slick."

"I'm not sure I like that one."

"Well, your nice opening pass was followed by you and your precious partner mentioning all four suits in rapid succession before making up your minds. Anyway, I was fingering the nine of clubs, when I remembered your saying that nines were dangerous opening leads, and twos almost as bad, because they

Game All; Dealer South

```
                 ♠ K 7 4 3
                 ♥ A Q
                 ♦ K Q 6 2
                 ♣ A K J
♠ Q 10 8 2                      ♠ J 6
♥ 10 7 6 2         N            ♥ K J 9 4 3
♦ 7 3          W     E          ♦ 8
♣ 9 8 3           S            ♣ Q 7 6 5 2
                 ♠ A 9 5
                 ♥ 8 5
                 ♦ A J 10 9 5 4
                 ♣ 10 4
```

revealed too much to declarer, and that a trump lead was recommended only against a *grand* slam. So back I went to the nine of clubs, which you won in dummy with the King. Then you drew trumps, I think, and played the King and Ace of spades, and I got quite excited, because I held the Queen and felt sure that you would switch and finesse through one of dummy's tenaces and be disappointed. Now why didn't you?"

"Because you and your partner had told me not to do so."

"When and how?"

"You were really very unlucky. Nines and twos are often the best opening leads. On this occasion your nine of clubs was the worst, while the two of hearts would have worked well. Your nine told me that you did *not* hold the Queen of clubs. Then at the third trick another nine, East's nine of hearts, which he discarded on the second round of trumps, told me that he *did* hold the King of hearts. So I knew, before I really started, that neither finesse would work, also that I could throw East in whenever I chose. So I played the two top spades as you said, and the Ace of clubs, to get them out of the way, and won the first six tricks. Now at the seventh trick I led dummy's Jack of clubs to East's Queen and *did not* ruff, but threw my last spade. This was the six-card end position:

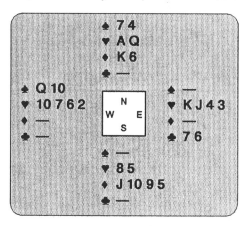

"Rather than lead a heart into dummy's tenace, East played a club and I discarded a heart from hand and ruffed in dummy."

"Suppose East had still held a spade?"

"I rather thought that he had, when I saw his Jack appear on the second round of the suit, and he would have led it, no doubt, in the diagram position. But you would have held one spade less, remember, so my ruff would have cleared the suit, establishing a winner in dummy, on which to throw a heart."

"Everything was wrong for you really – neither finesse was right, and the spades were not breaking – yet you sailed home. I wish I could play a hand like that!"

"Don't worry, you're doing fine. It wouldn't suit you yet to be canny, and I'd hate you to be slick!"

WAIT FOR IT

"Just when I thought we were improving," said my granddaughter. She was feeling disappointed at the end of a Pairs competition, in which she and young Bruce had finished equal bottom. "We didn't make a lot of mistakes, as far as we could see." She went on. "There was one board we still can't understand, so we wrote it down for you to see.

North	South
1♦	1♥
1♠	1NT
3NT	End

Game All; Dealer North

♠ K 7 5 3
♥ A 7 2
♦ A K Q 10
♣ 10 3

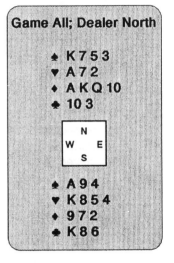

♠ A 9 4
♥ K 8 5 4
♦ 9 7 2
♣ K 8 6

"I think every pair was in three no-trumps, but at most tables it was played (and made) by North, but at ours played (and not made) by South (me)."

"I expect most Norths opened with one spade or a strong no-trump."

"Of the two Souths who played it, one made it (again not me). West led the four of clubs, East played the Queen, and I won with the King. There were eight tricks on top and three obvious chances of a ninth, one in each of the other three suits. What was I supposed to do about it?"

"Yes, I see your trouble. West might have led from five clubs and might now hold four club winners, so you couldn't afford to lose a diamond or to duck a round in one of the majors."

"I went straight for the diamonds, and, of course, they didn't break."

"I expect you ought to have waited. Why not exit at the second trick with another club? West may run four winners, but you would still hold your eight winners *and* know much more about the hand."

"But I would have to make three discards from dummy and two from my own hand."

"Yes, and East two from his. Let me see the hand."

"Before we go on, was East right to play the Queen of clubs on the first trick?"

"Yes, this was one of the stock occasions when you must finesse against

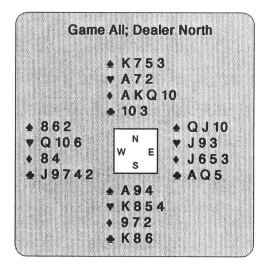

Game All; Dealer North

```
              ♠ K753
              ♥ A72
              ♦ AKQ10
              ♣ 103
♠ 862                        ♠ QJ10
♥ Q106        N              ♥ J93
♦ 84        W   E            ♦ J653
♣ J9742       S              ♣ AQ5
              ♠ A94
              ♥ K854
              ♦ 972
              ♣ K86
```

your partner in order to flush out the King, if South has it. What interests me is that the two major suits break evenly. Let's see how the discarding would go, if the club suit is run by West. Dummy can afford to lose two spades and one heart, and you can throw a heart and a diamond. However, East can't throw a diamond, so he will probably discard two hearts. After running all the clubs, West exits, say with a diamond, and South wins and tries running the suit but fails to drop the Jack. The expert South, of course, does all this in his head, but here's where you and I need a diagram. So I'm going to write down the position after eight tricks have been played, each side having won four of them. The lead is still in dummy, so King and Ace of hearts are played. I believe this is going to work. Yes, East is in trouble. He can't throw his Jack of diamonds on the second heart, so he's got to drop a spade and allow declarer to win three spade tricks and the contract."

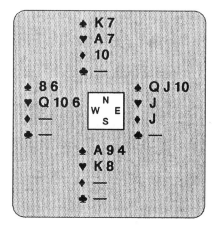

```
              ♠ K7
              ♥ A7
              ♦ 10
              ♣ —
♠ 86                      ♠ QJ10
♥ Q106      N             ♥ J
♦ —       W   E           ♦ J
♣ —         S             ♣ —
              ♠ A94
              ♥ K8
              ♦ —
              ♣ —
```

"Suppose West doesn't lead another club at the third trick."

"Then you win whatever he does lead and play another club yourself."

"Suppose West wins three clubs only, then switches."

"South can throw East in with a spade and set up an extra spade trick for himself."

"Shall I ever be able to squeeze anybody?"

"Of course. The first time or two it will be by accident – by just playing out winners, when you look like going one down."

"I certainly look like that often enough!"

PROMISING PAIR

"Bruce and I want to know," said my granddaughter, as she began to deal, "Whether we ought to aim high as a pair or keep it simple and middle-of-the-road."

"Bid high, play safe," I suggested.

"Or perhaps the other way round," said Paddy mischievously.

"Thanks very much. You're both a big help."

The middle of the road proved to be rather muddy, and they lost the first two rubbers, but they were a game up in the third, when I dealt this hand.

West	North	East	South
NB	1♣	1♥	1♠
2♥	4♠	End	

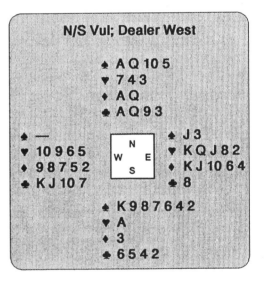

N/S Vul; Dealer West

♠ A Q 10 5
♥ 7 4 3
♦ A Q
♣ A Q 9 3

♠ —
♥ 10 9 6 5
♦ 9 8 7 5 2
♣ K J 10 7

♠ J 3
♥ K Q J 8 2
♦ K J 10 6 4
♣ 8

♠ K 9 8 7 6 4 2
♥ A
♦ 3
♣ 6 5 4 2

I led the Ten of hearts against Bruce's four spade contract. After winning with the Ace he thought for some time and at last, seeming to see his way ahead, he began to combine the drawing of trumps with the ruffing-out of both red suits. Having in this way won the first seven tricks, he led the two of clubs, on which I played the Ten. There was another long pause before he won (apparently to his surprise) with the Queen, continued with the Ace, conceded two club tricks, and to the delight of his partner claimed his contract with an overtrick. In spite of our congratulations he was not altogether happy.

"That didn't really go according to plan," he said.

"It was marvellous," remonstrated his partner. "I know I'd have taken the diamond finesse instead of doing that elimination."

"I wasn't really intending to finesse with either of the minor suit Queens, because the Kings were probably with East. When I led that club, I was going to play dummy's nine and throw East in, but his partner saw what I was at, and went up with the Ten."

"I was afraid that you might duck my Ten," I said "and win the rest of the clubs."

"I never thought of it. But was I right to start by eliminating both red suits?"

I just managed to check my enthusiastic "Of course you were" and listened to Paddy instead.

"Hearts, yes," he was saying, "but that diamond tenace in dummy might have been useful in one way or another. Suppose you eliminate hearts only, draw trumps and take a simple finesse of the club Queen. The point is that *if* the King of clubs is on your left, you make *twelve* tricks. You win with the Queen and play the Ace. If another club appears on your right, the suit must break, and you lose nothing but one club. If, as here, a discard appears, you play Ace and Queen of diamonds (you can be sure now that the missing King is on your right) and throw your opponent in. Look, here's the position after you have played the Ace of clubs and seen

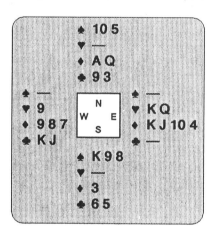

East's discard. You have won all seven tricks and now play Ace and Queen of diamonds throwing East in. You do *not* ruff his King but discard a club. He must now lead a red-suit card, on which you throw your last club, ruffing in dummy. You have lost nothing but the King of diamonds and have made twelve tricks in all."

"Beautiful," said my granddaughter.

"But beyond me," said Bruce.

"Now that you know twelve tricks are there, what does anyone think about the bidding?" asked Paddy.

"I suppose that I had more than I showed," said Bruce reluctantly.

"If you cue-bid five hearts, I can go six spades," said his partner eagerly.

"And *I* can go one down instead of making the rubber!"

"This is where we came in," I said, "Paddy and I were both wrong at the beginning. Partners are all the better for not being the same as each other. Carry on as you are, and you'll be a good pair!"

ANCIENT HISTORY

"Can you remember the best hand you ever held?" asked my granddaughter.

"I was a young man at the time, but it was such a historic hand . . ."

"Prehistoric, I'd say."

". . . that I recorded it and kept it."

"I'd love to see it."

"What's your idea of a perfect hand for a declarer?"

"Oh, a seven no-trump contract. Vulnerable. Doubled. 150 for Aces."

"A lay-down?"

"Certainly not. Requiring an elegant play (by me)."

"Just wait, while I find my hand. Promise not to be put off by the 'prehistoric' bidding. This was long before Acol.

South	North
3NT	6NT
7NT	End

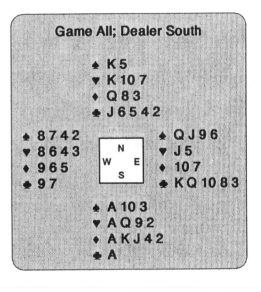

Game All; Dealer South

```
            ♠ K 5
            ♥ K 10 7
            ♦ Q 8 3
            ♣ J 6 5 4 2
♠ 8 7 4 2              ♠ Q J 9 6
♥ 8 6 4 3      N       ♥ J 5
♦ 9 6 5    W     E     ♦ 10 7
♣ 9 7         S        ♣ K Q 10 8 3
            ♠ A 10 3
            ♥ A Q 9 2
            ♦ A K J 4 2
            ♣ A
```

"I was South. I dealt and played this hand, which was not doubled but seems otherwise just right for you. A little thing like a singleton Ace didn't rule out no-trumps in those days, so I opened with three (a modern pair would, of course, sail into a dull lay-down contract of seven diamonds). My cheerful partner tried six, and, as I had never been in seven of anything before, I took my opportunity. In passing, may I remind you of my dislike of today's Gambling Three No-trump opening bid? I even prefer this one. Anyhow, what do you think of my chances here of making the grand slam?"

"I can't see more than twelve tricks. Those were certainly the days. What happened?"

"West had no idea what to lead from his yarborough, and made the horrible choice of the two of spades, which I let run and won with the Ace over East's Jack. With no real plan, I reeled off five diamonds and three top hearts, and reached this position with a fourth heart winner, the nine, still to play:

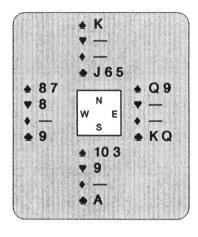

"On my nine of hearts, drawing West's eight, I discarded a club from dummy, and East threw the *King* of clubs. Now came the biggest crisis of my bridge life. Did West, I asked myself, hold both black Queens or only one? It never occurred to me that he might hold neither! All I had to do, you can see, was lead my Ace of clubs and win the last two tricks in dummy. All I actually did was lead a spade, in the hope that West's last three cards were the Queen of spades and the Queen-nine of clubs. Perhaps you can see what would have happened if I had been right, and what did happen when I got it wrong."

"Yes, I can see. What a shame. Poor you!"

"I think West's lucky opening lead was partly to blame, since it put the idea of his holding a spade honour firmly into my head, but I remember being suspicious of East's discard of the King of clubs, as we all false-carded madly. Some thirty years later I was told that I had contrived what is called a criss-cross squeeze on East. I have been looking for another ever since and, as far as I know, have never again been near one. Anyhow, it all goes to make a good story."

"I do wish it had had a happy ending."

"Then nobody, not even my granddaughter, would have believed me!"

NO JOKE

"I tried to bring off an endplay," said my granddaughter.

"You certainly succeeded," answered her partner, Bruce.

All four of us considered this exchange briefly, then found that it was really very funny and began to laugh. This is what had just happened.

East	South	West	North
NB	1♥	NB	4♥

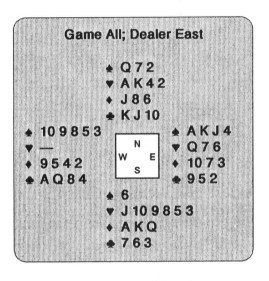

Game All; Dealer East

```
              ♠ Q 7 2
              ♥ A K 4 2
              ♦ J 8 6
              ♣ K J 10
♠ 10 9 8 5 3            ♠ A K J 4
♥ —           N          ♥ Q 7 6
♦ 9 5 4 2  W     E       ♦ 10 7 3
♣ A Q 8 4     S          ♣ 9 5 2
              ♠ 6
              ♥ J 10 9 8 5 3
              ♦ A K Q
              ♣ 7 6 3
```

Against her four heart contract, West (my partner, Paddy) had led the Ten of spades, overtaken by my Jack, which was followed by my King. She had ruffed and led the Jack of hearts and had been momentarily upset when West discarded a spade. But soon, as she now explained, she had found herself not really minding this distribution and even welcoming it, because it gave her a chance to distinguish herself. She would not risk leading clubs, she would simply play Ace and King of trumps, ruff out dummy's last spade, play three rounds of diamonds, and throw me (East) in with a third trump to my Queen. I would then have to choose between giving her a ruff and discard, and leading a club towards dummy's honours.

"I still don't understand what went wrong," she protested now. "Please let's just put out the cards as they were at the end. After losing the first trick, I had ruffed the second, won the next six and thrown my grandfather in at the ninth. He didn't seem to mind much, which was disappointing. What exactly was the position at that point?"

"Actually," I said, "I didn't at all like having to lead a club, and thought you had been clever."

"So did I," said Bruce, "until West unkindly ducked and let the club run to dummy's Ten!"

"After that unfair play," went on my granddaughter, "I wasn't going to lead

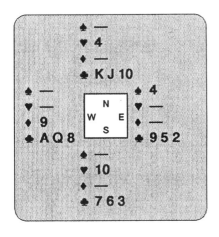

another club from dummy, so I returned with a trump to my own hand . . ."

"And West coolly discarded his Queen of clubs and won the last two tricks with the Ace of clubs and the nine of diamonds."

". . . and all I had done was endplay myself!"

There was further amusement, not without a mention of the club's annual brilliancy prize, before we came back to earth.

"Of course, it's obvious now," said my granddaughter, "that all I had to do, as the cards lay, was to lead clubs twice from my hand, but what I really want to know is how the odds against a club finesse compare with those against a throw-in play."

"I'm not sure you're going to like the answer to your question," said Paddy, to whom we usually refer the more difficult points arising at the bridge table, "but, as I'm in the dog-house already, I'll tell you what I think. First, I believe that you were put off by the bad distribution and forgot the auction. My partner could not find a bid, yet he had shown no fewer than ten points in the play of the first three tricks – what clearer proof do you want that he did not hold either club honour? Second, I think you'll find that a throw-in play could never work here, however the opposing clubs lie. Give East both Ace and Queen, if you like, he can always make them both by exiting with another card, even another club."

"I see. So I had a choice between a 100% certainty and a 0% chance and carefully chose the latter? That is no laughing matter." She paused. "Or is it?" she added, and we were off again.

DUMMY RUN

Just as I was going out, my granddaughter appeared. "I'll come back later," she said.

"No, don't go. I've got five minutes, and that looks like a bridge diagram."

"It's really only a bidding question. Suppose you deal yourself one of the best hands you've ever seen! ♠ A 7 6 5 ♥ A K 9 ♦ A K 5 3 ♣ A 7 – surely just too good for two no trumps, so you open with two clubs. Your partner says *three* diamonds. What do you bid? Rubber bridge, remember."

"Four diamonds. There's no hurry . . . I see you don't agree, so I'm going to make a quick guess as to who the bidder was – you. And as to what you bid – seven diamonds."

"Aren't you clever? You're not quite right, however. I thought of four possible bids in this order, four no-trumps (Blackwood), four diamonds (your bid), four hearts (cue bid) and seven diamonds. Then I suddenly panicked, scrapped the lot and said seven no-trumps!"

"There's much to be said for it. What happened?"

"West led the eight of hearts, and these were the cards. As you see, there were twelve tricks on top in either no-trumps or diamonds, but no thirteenth."

"Seven diamonds (by North) looks much the better contract, I'm afraid. Do you mind if I show off a little by saying that it has a nearly 70% chance of success?"

"How do you make that out?"

"There is a 68-point-something-per-cent chance of the opponents' spades being divided 3-2, in which case declarer (North) could throw two spades on South's high hearts, ruff a third spade and establish a fourth on which to throw a losing club." I was beginning to feel rather pleased with myself. "Whereas," I went on, "in seven no-trumps there's only the fantastically remote chance of a squeeze on an opponent holding all the important defence cards. Show me the hand."

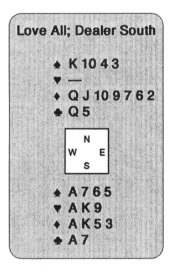

Love All; Dealer South

♠ K 10 4 3
♥ —
♦ Q J 10 9 7 6 2
♣ Q 5

```
      N
   W     E
      S
```

♠ A 7 6 5
♥ A K 9
♦ A K 5 3
♣ A 7

South	North
2♣	3♦
7NT	End

"I might have known it, the spades are 4-1! So much for my famous 68%. Well, at least, you had one thing to console you, 150 for Aces. I suppose you went one down."

"Yes, I threw a club and a spade on the Ace and King of hearts and had to lose a spade at the end."

"Just a minute, let me look at that hand again . . . Good heavens, how extraordinary! I didn't really look at East's cards before. Do you see what I see?"

Love All; Dealer South

```
                ♠ K 10 4 3
                ♥ —
                ♦ Q J 10 9 7 6 2
                ♣ Q 5
♠ J                          ♠ Q 9 8 2
♥ 8 7 6 5 4 2    N           ♥ Q J 10 3
♦ 8 4          W   E         ♦ —
♣ J 9 6 2        S           ♣ K 10 8 4 3
                ♠ A 7 6 5
                ♥ A K 9
                ♦ A K 5 3
                ♣ A 7
```

"What's wrong? He's got thirteen cards."

"Including all the ones that matter. Don't you realise that, whether the contract is in no-trumps or diamonds, he has to find no fewer that *seven* discards on dummy's long diamond suit? I'm sure he can't possibly do it. Declarer won't be in any difficulty because his three discards come after East's. Have you ever squeezed anybody?"

"I wouldn't know how."

"Try this one and give yourself a treat, squeezing this East of yours. I really have got to go now, but do see what happens when you run all those diamonds. Would you like to try what is called a Vienna Coup? After winning the opening heart, just remember to play the Ace of clubs before you start on the diamonds. You may see why later on. If you feel strong enough, do one of your beautiful diagrams to show the end position – five-card position, I think – with one diamond still to go, and I'll frame it together with the full deal. What shall we call it? 'My First Squeeze'?"

"What about 'Dummy Run'?"

OVERDOING IT

The old stagers had lost the first three rubbers and looked like losing the fourth and last, in which their young opponents at game all had won 40 in the final game. It was at this point that I dealt and opened one diamond. I am not proud of my next bid. These were our cards and this was the auction:

North	South
1♦	1♠
2♥	3NT

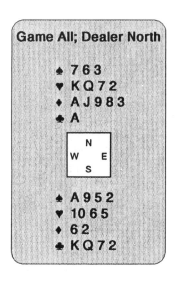

Game All; Dealer North

♠ 7 6 3
♥ K Q 7 2
♦ A J 9 8 3
♣ A

♠ A 9 5 2
♥ 10 6 5
♦ 6 2
♣ K Q 7 2

West (my granddaughter) led the Jack of clubs, and South (my partner, Paddy) saw that he had problems. My light-hearted reverse into hearts had suggested more power than I really possessed, and there were obvious communication difficulties.

Paddy decided, as he told us later, to try to get more information, possibly even some assistance, by making a surprise lead at trick two – dummy's two of hearts, which ran to his own Ten and West's Ace. Now came another club to his Queen which allowed him to try a deep diamond finesse of dummy's eight. East (young Bruce) won with the Queen and led a third club. Now declarer could win with the King, take a second diamond finesse, find both red suits breaking evenly and make the rest of the tricks. With four diamonds, three hearts, three clubs and one spade, he had made two overtricks!

Somebody had to say something, so I broke the silence. "That was lucky," I said. "I should never have reversed into hearts. I ought to have said two spades or just two diamonds."

"In which case," said Paddy, "I call two no-trumps and you pass."

"I'm sorry to be stupid," put in my granddaughter, "but you seem to be saying that you ought not to have been in a game contract, and yet you got two overtricks."

"I'm afraid," Bruce told her, "that I made a nonsense of the defence by not going up with the Jack of hearts at trick two. How could I have told?"

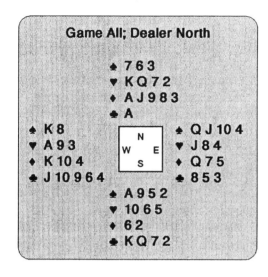

Game All; Dealer North

```
                ♠ 7 6 3
                ♥ K Q 7 2
                ♦ A J 9 8 3
                ♣ A
  ♠ K 8              N        ♠ Q J 10 4
  ♥ A 9 3        W       E    ♥ J 8 4
  ♦ K 10 4           S        ♦ Q 7 5
  ♣ J 10 9 6 4                ♣ 8 5 3
                ♠ A 9 5 2
                ♥ 10 6 5
                ♦ 6 2
                ♣ K Q 7 2
```

"Didn't dummy's hearts show you," I asked, "that you could have no possible use for the Jack later on?"

"There was rather more wrong with the defence than just that," said Paddy. "Somebody on my left ought not to have let me run all those diamonds like that. You ought to have gone up with the King on the first round," he explained to my granddaughter, "then I'd have been in trouble, since the easy establishment of the suit would have been blocked. By the way, when you won the second trick with the Ace of hearts, did it occur to you that you might switch from clubs? Your partner's three of clubs at the first trick was not encouraging. Why not try the King of spades?"

"But that was your suit!"

"You ought to know Paddy's suits by this time," I told her.

"Yes, but all that wouldn't have mattered," said Bruce gallantly, "if I had played my Jack of hearts at trick two. What would have happened against best defence?"

"I think," said Paddy, "That best defence by both of you holds me to six tricks – three down."

"Of course," said my granddaughter thoughtfully to her partner, "we had to let them win one rubber, but presenting them with five tricks in one hand was a little ostentatious!"

NO MARKS

"You know those bridge competitions in the papers which ask you to award marks out of ten to certain bids or leads or plays," said my granddaughter. "Would you mind if I gave you a small play problem and ask you which of three cards you would give the most marks to, and how many to the other two?"

"I'll have a shot at it. Is this rubber bridge?"

"No, pairs, actually. Here are the two hands and an auction. West leads the Jack of clubs against South's three no-trumps. Which card should South play from dummy?"

South	North
1NT	3NT

"Am I allowed to award all ten points to one card?"

"Yes, I suppose so, if you think there's nothing to be said for playing either of the other two."

I thought for a little while. "I don't think you're going to like this," I said at last, "I'm giving eight points to the Ace of clubs, one to the Queen, one to the six."

"Yes, you *have* rather torn it. How did you know I wouldn't much like your answer?"

"I guessed that someone, probably you, played the Queen, and that East won and cleared the club suit. Then, I supposed, South lost the diamond finesse and five of the first six tricks."

Game All; Dealer South

```
        ♠ A 9 5 4
        ♥ 10 7 2
        ♦ 10 6 2
        ♣ A Q 6
            N
        W       E
            S
        ♠ K 8 7
        ♥ A J
        ♦ A K J 9 5
        ♣ 8 7 3
```

"You're much too clever. Actually South was Bruce, not me, last night at the club, and that's exactly what happened. Can you honestly tell me that you would have given those marks, even if you hadn't guessed that one of us was South? Suppose you had simply seen the question in a magazine."

"Then I think I'd have made it 10–0–0, instead of 8–1–1! What marks did you and Bruce decide on and why?"

"We thought 5–5–0, and what we really wanted was a casting vote from you. We've got it all right! We reckoned that South had eight tricks on top and needed one of the two minor suit finesses for the ninth, and that the opening lead had forced him to try the club finesse first, if he tried it at all.

We also saw that both finesses would have to be right in order to get the overtrick. We did see, however, that it might be best to keep control at the first trick, and that playing the Queen was risky. When we later found out that most pairs made the no-trump game, we knew we must have forgotten something."

"When you hear what that something was, you'll kick yourselves. If the club finesse would succeed, it isn't necessary! That sounds cryptic, but the point is that if the King is with West, the Queen will be a winner later, when the suit is led again (and South can lead it himself, if needed). That is really enough to gain all ten marks for the play of the Ace at the first trick. Other smaller advantages include the possibility of East having the singleton King, and the need to guard South's other weak suit, hearts. A heart lead from West wouldn't matter, but from East it might be damaging – in fact, I originally awarded one mark for playing the six of clubs, because at least it would leave the lead in West's hand."

"What about one mark for the Queen, which you later withdrew?"

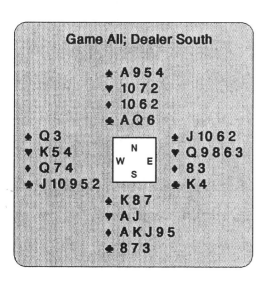

Game All; Dealer South

♠ A 9 5 4
♥ 10 7 2
♦ 10 6 2
♣ A Q 6

♠ Q 3
♥ K 5 4
♦ Q 7 4
♣ J 10 9 5 2

N
W E
S

♠ J 10 6 2
♥ Q 9 8 6 3
♦ 8 3
♣ K 4

♠ K 8 7
♥ A J
♦ A K J 9 5
♣ 8 7 3

"It's the simplest, easiest, laziest card to play, and might get you home with least trouble! Show me the whole hand. Ah, yes, I see. Bruce could have won with the Ace of clubs, taken the diamond finesse losing to West, had the sense not to cover the next club lead, and made his contract with four diamonds, two clubs, two spades and one heart. Where are you off to?"

"I'm just going to go across the road to report to Bruce. If you hear a lot of noise, it'll be me kicking him."

"What I actually said was 'Kick *yourselves*' – plural."

"Oh, he'd never kick me!"

BY CHANCE

Paddy had rung to say he would be half-an-hour late for our rubber bridge. "While we're waiting," I told my granddaughter, "you'd better solve my insoluble bridge problem. Last week, when I was partnering Paddy, I made ten tricks when there were only nine there."

"That's unlike you."

"Thanks."

"I mean it's unlike you to boast. There's a catch somewhere."

"I think I can remember the very ordinary looking hand. Just let me write down the North-South cards and the auction."

"Was this rubber bridge?"

"Yes. West started with the three top clubs against my four spade contract. Now if you look carefully, you'll see that I had five possible winners – two hearts and three diamonds – outside trumps. You'll find later that I could *not* have caught the King of diamonds, which was with East, and I could *not* have dropped the Queen and Jack of trumps. I was bound to lose two clubs and one diamond, so must not lose a trump. Impossible, don't you agree?"

West	North	East	South
1♣	Dbl	NB	2♠
NB	4♠	End	

Love All; Dealer West

```
        ♠ A 10 6
        ♥ A K 7 4
        ♦ A 9
        ♣ 8 7 4 3
              N
          W       E
              S
        ♠ K 9 8 7 4
        ♥ 10 8
        ♦ Q J 10 8
        ♣ J 5
```

"Not if you make an opponent lead trumps first."

"Good point, but there was no throwing-in to be done except with a diamond to East's King, and he could always exit with another diamond."

"Well then, someone must have revoked."

"Nothing so sensational, I'm afraid. Everything proceeded in an orderly way. Before I show you the whole hand and tell you what happened, I want to make it clear that I was hardly responsible. I suppose I can take some credit for knowing that the most probable distribution of the opposing spades was 3-2 with divided honours, and perhaps my play was to that extent instinctive, but I had no plan and, at one point, no hope. Anyhow, here's the deal.

"I ruffed West's third club lead and ran the Queen of diamonds to East, who won with the King and returned another diamond to the Ace. I had lost three tricks and had to win the rest. I ruffed the last club, played Ace and King of hearts, ruffed a heart and led the established Jack of diamonds. West did not ruff, as this would not have helped him, and this was the position. Now I led the eight of diamonds, ruffed by West and overruffed in dummy. Look at what's left.

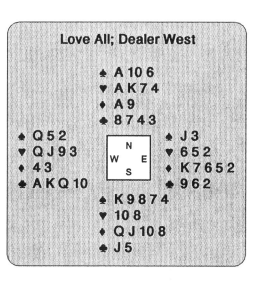

Love All; Dealer West

♠ A 10 6
♥ A K 7 4
♦ A 9
♣ 8 7 4 3

♠ Q 5 2   ♠ J 3
♥ Q J 9 3   ♥ 6 5 2
♦ 4 3   ♦ K 7 6 5 2
♣ A K Q 10   ♣ 9 6 2

♠ K 9 8 7 4
♥ 10 8
♦ Q J 10 8
♣ J 5

"For the first time in my life, I imagine, I found myself drawing trumps at the twelfth trick with the Ace and the King! You remember that it seemed at one time impossible to make five trump tricks. I had won *six*."

"What did you say at the time?"

"Nothing"

"What did the others say?"

"Nothing. Two of them, strangers, perhaps thought 'Wise old bird'. One of them, Paddy, almost certainly thought 'Lucky old so-and-so'."

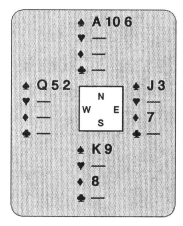

♠ A 10 6
♥ —
♦ —
♣ —

♠ Q 5 2   ♠ J 3
♥ —   ♥ —
♦ —   ♦ 7
♣ —   ♣ —

♠ K 9
♥ —
♦ 8
♣ —

OPENING TIME

My granddaughter was indignant with me. "We had only twenty-two points between us," she protested.

"Yes, I'm sorry about that. All the same . . ."

"Oh dear. I don't like the sound of 'all the same'."

We had been partners at the club and had been doing well, apart from one rather expensive last rubber. My partner had gone two down twice running in game contracts, and we were recalling the first of them which had been doubled.

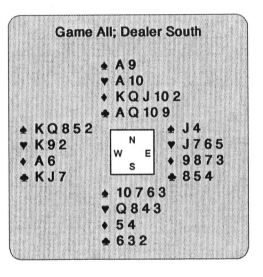

South	West	North	East
NB	1♠	Dbl	NB
2♥	NB	2♠	NB
2NT	NB	3NT	NB
NB	Dbl	End	

Game All; Dealer South

```
                    ♠ A 9
                    ♥ A 10
                    ♦ K Q J 10 2
                    ♣ A Q 10 9
   ♠ K Q 8 5 2              ♠ J 4
   ♥ K 9 2          N       ♥ J 7 6 5
   ♦ A 6        W     E     ♦ 9 8 7 3
   ♣ K J 7          S       ♣ 8 5 4
                    ♠ 10 7 6 3
                    ♥ Q 8 4 3
                    ♦ 5 4
                    ♣ 6 3 2
```

She was South, and West had opened with the five of spades, which was ducked and won by East's Jack. Another spade went to dummy's Ace, and the King of diamonds was led. West won and ran three spade winners, on which were thrown a heart and two clubs from dummy. Now a heart to dummy's bare Ace gave West a final winner, the King of clubs.

"You could tell from West's opening five of spades," I went on now," that East must have a spade honour. Agree?"

"I suppose so . . . In which case I ought to have gone up with the Ace at the first trick. Is that it?"

"Yes. If East plays the Jack under it, your Ten becomes an eventual winner. If he plays low, the suit is blocked, at any rate for the time being. You would give them the chance to go wrong. But I do admit that my bidding was a bit off."

"Not as bad as mine in the next hand. I *knew* I ought to have kept my mouth shut. I just couldn't resist saying something, and then found myself swept into game."

"All the same . . ."

"Oh *no*. Not again. I can't bear it!"

West	North	East	South
1♠	2♦	NB	2♥
NB	2NT	NB	3♥
NB	4♥	End	

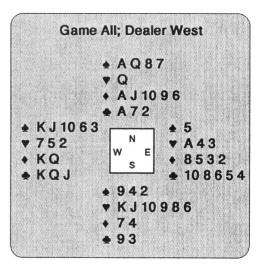

Game All; Dealer West

```
            ♠ A Q 8 7
            ♥ Q
            ♦ A J 10 9 6
            ♣ A 7 2
♠ K J 10 6 3              ♠ 5
♥ 7 5 2          N       ♥ A 4 3
♦ K Q         W     E    ♦ 8 5 3 2
♣ K Q J          S       ♣ 10 8 6 5 4
            ♠ 9 4 2
            ♥ K J 10 9 8 6
            ♦ 7 4
            ♣ 9 3
```

This time West had led the King of clubs, won in dummy. East had won the heart lead and surprised everybody by playing the five of spades next. However, South's delight soon vanished, when she realised that she was locked in dummy, unable to draw trumps. Whatever she did (actually she tried Ace and another diamond), West must win, give his partner a spade ruff and prevent South from winning more than eight tricks, five trumps, two minor-suit Aces and the Queen of spades.

"What was I supposed to do about it?" she asked now.

"You might have seen the danger of a shift to spades and a spade ruff (after all we held seven spades between us, and West had bid the suit) and made sure that you had an entry to your hand by leading another club immediately at the second trick."

"I see. Is that what you would have done yourself?"

"No, I think (I hope) that I would have simply ducked the first trick, leaving the lead with West."

"So it was really another first-trick crisis. Last time I ducked when I shouldn't, this time I should have ducked. I was just unlucky both times."

"I think you were *lucky* both times – in having enough honest evidence before even playing to the first trick."

"Yes. *And* in having an honest grandfather!"

SUPPORTING PARTNER

My granddaughter was feeling annoyed with herself. She had been losing during most of the evening's rubber bridge with Bruce as her partner and at the end she had had to make the opening lead at Game All against my four spade contract. She had not made a happy choice.

"Why did you pick on your singleton trump?" asked Bruce, sounding rather unlike his usual uncritical self.

"Because I was void in your suit. Look, this is what I held:

♠ 6 ♥ K 9 7 6 5 3 ♦ A Q 9 6 5 2 ♣ None

"Also, I had no help from the auction. After your opening three clubs came declarer's four spades. A lead from either red-card suit might have been fatal."

"Ace and another diamond would have been fatal for them."

"Whose side are you on, anyhow?"

"She certainly had a problem," put in my partner, Paddy. "Let's look at the whole hand."

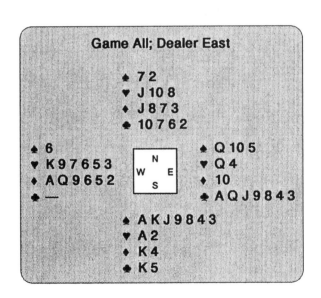

Game All; Dealer East

	♠ 7 2	
	♥ J 10 8	
	♦ J 8 7 3	
	♣ 10 7 6 2	
♠ 6		♠ Q 10 5
♥ K 9 7 6 5 3	N W E S	♥ Q 4
♦ A Q 9 6 5 2		♦ 10
♣ —		♣ A Q J 9 8 4 3
	♠ A K J 9 8 4 3	
	♥ A 2	
	♦ K 4	
	♣ K 5	

East	South	West	North
3♣	4♠	End	

48

I had been South and was hoping to call two spades when Bruce forestalled me with an opening of three clubs. I could think of nothing better than four spades, and my granddaughter on my left became a picture of frustration (I find her naturalness at the table refreshing, however unethical), put her cards face down on the table, consulted the ceiling, and at last, probably for the first time in her life, said "I pass," which was followed by two more normal 'no-bids'. Now came another long pause and the disputed lead of the six of spades.

"Your lead happened to be very lucky for me," I explained to her, "not just because it solved my trump problem for me, it also told me that you had a club void and probably found both red-card suits unattractive to lead from. I could guess that you held the Ace and Queen of diamonds and the King of hearts. Then when I drew trumps and you discarded on the second trick, I could suspect the whole lay-out. That's why after drawing trumps I led the King of diamonds. I knew you could make two diamond tricks but would have to switch sooner or later to a heart."

Paddy turned to my granddaughter. "Do you remember which heart you led?" he asked. "It was at the sixth trick."

"The six, I think."

"Which went to your partner's Queen and declarer's Ace. Now came the unkind lead of another heart, and you had to go up with the King."

"Yes, and lead another red-suit card to one of dummy's horrible Jacks, both of which had become established, so we never won another trick."

"Go back to the sixth trick. Why did you not lead the *King* of hearts?"

"It looks an absolutely crazy lead."

"Yet it would have made declarer as uncomfortable as he made you. He would win with the Ace and have to put Bruce in with the Queen to lead his Ace of clubs and down the contract."

"Suppose," I interrupted unwisely "that I simply duck her King of hearts lead. Then Bruce never gets in."

"Doesn't he? She simply exits with another heart to your Ace, and at the end *you* have to lead a club into his tenace and go *two* down!"

"And whose side are *you* on?" I asked.

At least I seemed to have cheered everybody up.

QUESTION TIME

"It's not that I didn't know the right answers," my granddaughter told me, "apparently I don't even know the right questions." She had returned, rather subdued, from partnering Bruce in rubber bridge at the club and had spent the last five minutes in constructing two diagrams for me to see.

"We were playing against old Carter and his wife," she explained, "and North (Bruce) dealt this hand at Game All and opened with one no-trump and then bid three no-trumps over my three spades, We are supposed to play Gerber, but each of us suspects the other of forgetting, so we usually bypass it. That's why I jumped to six and found myself doubled by West (Mrs Carter). These were our cards. West led the eight of diamonds. I knew, of course, that she must hold all, or nearly all, the missing high honour cards, including the Queen of trumps and the King of hearts. I could catch the former, I hoped, but was bound to lose the latter. Agree?"

North	East	South	West
1NT	NB	3♠	NB
3NT	NB	6♠	Dbl
End			

Game All; Dealer North

> ♠ A 9
> ♥ Q J 6
> ♦ K Q J
> ♣ 10 8 5 3 2

```
      N
  W       E
      S
```

> ♠ K J 10 8 7 6 3
> ♥ A 10
> ♦ A 9 5
> ♣ K

"It certainly looks like it. What happened?"

"That happened. I won the diamond lead in dummy, led a club to West's Ace, won the second diamond in hand and successfully finessed dummy's nine of trumps. Now I could draw trumps without loss, but had to go down when the King of hearts duly turned up on my left. By the way, do I talk too much at the bridge table?"

"No – just about the right amount, in my opinion. There are too many grim players about these days. Why?"

"Old Carter didn't seem to like me explaining to Bruce that I hadn't a chance. Perhaps I did go on a bit. Anyhow, he said something about my not having asked myself how many entries there were to dummy. What on earth had that to do with anything? And I do *not* care for being addressed as 'young lady.' Oh, and then he went on to say something about a percentage figure – 62%, I think it was – but I had no idea what he was talking about. He suddenly switched off and began criticising his wife instead and saying that her double had told me how to play the hand

– not that she seemed to mind, I expect she's used to him by now."

"He's a very good player, you know. That percentage figure seems familiar to me somehow. I believe it's a distributional-odds figure. Yes, I remember, it tells you the odds on seven cards of a suit being divided 4-3. Show me the whole hand.

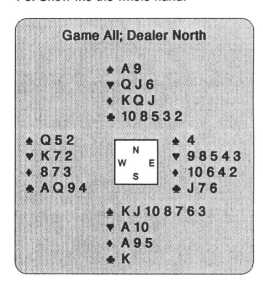

Game All; Dealer North

```
                ♠ A 9
                ♥ Q J 6
                ♦ K Q J
                ♣ 10 8 5 3 2
   ♠ Q 5 2                      ♠ 4
   ♥ K 7 2          N           ♥ 9 8 5 4 3
   ♦ 8 7 3       W     E        ♦ 10 6 4 2
   ♣ A Q 9 4        S           ♣ J 7 6
                ♠ K J 10 8 7 6 3
                ♥ A 10
                ♦ A 9 5
                ♣ K
```

"Yes, I see . . . I wonder whether . . . I believe I've got it. I think he was telling you that you could have known that the unseen clubs were probably divided 4-3. If you had counted your entries to dummy, you would have found that there were four, two in trumps (almost certainly) and two in diamonds – enough for you to ruff three clubs and cross to win with the last club, on which to throw your losing heart. Only you had to be careful not to waste an entry and must therefore win the opening diamond lead with your Ace, not in dummy, and lead the King of clubs. Then, with careful timing, you can combine the establishing and playing of the ten of clubs with the finessing of dummy's nine of trumps and the drawing of trumps, and there's your contract. You lose nothing but one club."

"I hereby apologise to old Carter. If he calls me 'young lady' again, I can always take a deep breath and call him 'old man'. So good luck to him – and even more to Mrs Carter!"

BOOK LEARNING

"People who write books about bridge," said my granddaughter, "are always telling me to 'plan the play' as soon as dummy's cards go down. It's difficult enough for declarers, but apparently defenders ought to do it as well."

"I suppose they ought to try. Occasionally there's enough evidence to go on from the auction and opening lead . . . Just a minute, let's see whether you do better than I did on one of the boards I had to play this afternoon. I think I can remember it. I'll do a small diagram:

East	South	West	North
1♦	4♠	End	

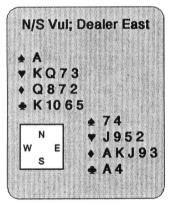

N/S Vul; Dealer East

♠ A
♥ K Q 7 3
♦ Q 8 7 2
♣ K 10 6 5

♠ 7 4
♥ J 9 5 2
♦ A K J 9 3
♣ A 4

"I was East. Imagine yourself in my place, feeling rather annoyed by South's jump bid. Your partner's opening lead against the four spade contract is the six of diamonds. You win with the Jack and continue with the King, all following. What do you lead next?"

"Another diamond, of course. My partner might be able to overruff or have one of his trumps promoted. It seems so obvious that I suppose I must be wrong. I'd lead the three of diamonds and hope for a club return."

"That is exactly what I did and for exactly the same reasons, and I've been regretting it ever since. I didn't attempt to 'plan the play'. Nor did you."

"I can't see anything to plan. I've got three tricks in my hand and my partner has just got to provide another."

"Neither you or I bothered to wonder what South held. After all, his explosive bid was evidence of a sort."

"Well, may I start wondering now? First, how many spades has he got? At least seven, probably more, as he's not got the Ace. He also hasn't got any of the high minor-suit honours. He must have something apart from spades. I'll give him the Ace of hearts, for a start. How am I doing?"

"Better than your grandfather. Go on."

"South can't have more than eleven or twelve points. *Four* spades, he calls. I'll give him *eight* spades, the Ace of hearts, two diamonds (that's for sure) and two other cards – say one more heart and one club."

"Loud applause!"

"Thank you, but I still can't see how all this affects East's lead at the third trick. I still think a diamond is best and safest."

"Suppose that an evil-minded South, rather than promote a trump in West's hand, refuses to ruff the third diamond."

"Then West ruffs and downs the contract."

"West did ruff. He did *not* down the contract. Look."

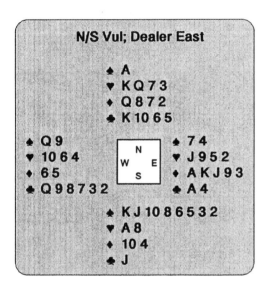

N/S Vul; Dealer East

♠ A
♥ K Q 7 3
♦ Q 8 7 2
♣ K 10 6 5

♠ Q 9
♥ 10 6 4
♦ 6 5
♣ Q 9 8 7 3 2

♠ 7 4
♥ J 9 5 2
♦ A K J 9 3
♣ A 4

♠ K J 10 8 6 5 3 2
♥ A 8
♦ 10 4
♣ J

"Yes, that's just what I said South had . . . Oh, I *see* – he must have thrown his singleton Jack of clubs on the third trick, so you never made your Ace. You really were very unlucky!"

"All I had to do was play the Ace of clubs before leading the third diamond. Like you I saw at once that the best chance was to promote a trump in West's hand by leading that diamond. There was no excuse for me. After all, what could I lose by making the club trick first?"

"Suppose South had had a club void. You'd have looked silly then."

"In that case there would have been no hope whatever of defeating the contract. You've got to assume on these occasions that the right cards are in the right places."

"That's funny. My book says that you've got to expect the *worst*. It's all very difficult."

"Only at the table. Not if you're writing a book!"

BALANCING ACT

"Paddy was at it again last night," I told my granddaughter. "That's why we nearly won the match."

"*You* must have been 'at it' as well."

"I was – that's why we lost."

"My grandfather is talking nonsense again, and I won't have it."

"Which would you like to see first, Paddy's good defence or my idiotic declarer play?"

"I'm sure it was *not* idiotic, just some small slip, so let's have it first."

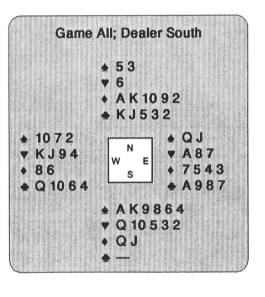

South	North
1♠	2♦
2♥	3♣
3♠	4♠

Game All; Dealer South

```
              ♠ 5 3
              ♥ 6
              ♦ A K 10 9 2
              ♣ K J 5 3 2
♠ 10 7 2                    ♠ Q J
♥ K J 9 4      N            ♥ A 8 7
♦ 8 6        W   E          ♦ 7 5 4 3
♣ Q 10 6 4     S            ♣ A 9 8 7
              ♠ A K 9 8 6 4
              ♥ Q 10 5 3 2
              ♦ Q J
              ♣ —
```

"I was South, declarer in a four spade contract, and West led the two of trumps. It looked like a lay-down with five trumps and five diamonds – until I realised that, once dummy's trumps were gone, I might lose as many as three hearts. Telling myself that at worst it depended on the position of the Jack of hearts, a 50% chance, I decided to risk it and drew trumps, losing the third round to West's Ten. He led a small heart, and I was one down."

"What could you have done?"

"Simply duck the first trick! A 100% chance!"

"Yes, I think I see that now. Oh, that was just one of those blind-spot things that experts are supposed to have occasionally, it wasn't what I call a mistake! Let's look at the other hand."

"This time I was West. I opened with the five of spades against South's four hearts. The Jack was played from dummy, and East (Paddy) followed with the Ten. South now ran the three of hearts to the six, Jack and King, and I was in again. What was I to make of Paddy's Ten of spades on the first trick?"

"It must have been a singleton."

"Then South must have held five, yet he did not support his partner's suit."

"Then it was a suit preference signal, asking for a diamond."

Love All; Dealer North

```
            ♠ K Q J 8 6
            ♥ Q 10 8 3
            ♦ A K
            ♣ Q J
♠ 5 3        ┌─────────┐
♥ K 9 4      │    N    │
♦ J 8 6 3    │  W   E  │
♣ A 9 7 3    │    S    │
            └─────────┘
```

North	South
1♠	2♥
4♥	End

"Almost impossible. Look at dummy's diamonds. No, I came to the conclusion that Paddy must want another spade. Now look at the whole hand."

Love All; Dealer North

```
            ♠ K Q J 8 6
            ♥ Q 10 8 3
            ♦ A K
            ♣ Q J
♠ 5 3        ┌─────────┐   ♠ A 10 2
♥ K 9 4      │    N    │   ♥ 6
♦ J 8 6 3    │  W   E  │   ♦ 10 9 7 4
♣ A 9 7 3    │    S    │   ♣ 10 8 5 4 2
            └─────────┘
            ♠ 9 7 4
            ♥ A J 7 5 2
            ♦ Q 5 2
            ♣ K 6
```

"Yes, I see. He *was* asking for another spade. He had the Ace all the time. I still don't understand why he didn't win the first trick with it . . . Oh yes, I do! He wanted to win the second round and give you a ruff on the third round."

"Yes, he thought I was more likely to hold a doubleton spade than a singleton. So do you think I led another spade at the third trick? Well I didn't! I made him wait just a moment while I played my Ace of clubs, before any rats got at it. Then came the spade to his Ace and the spade ruff, and we had South down. In the other room the opening lead was a diamond, and our South had no trouble."

"That was clever of Paddy, but cleverer of you. Paddy knows that he can make these mystery plays and that you will understand what's happening."

"All right, so now I'm going to confess. I would have kept quiet about that first hand, if I hadn't felt rather proud of the second!"

CAUTIONARY TALE

"Would you think it possible," I asked my granddaughter, "for any declarer to know the complete distribution of a hand and the position of all the significant cards before even playing to the first trick?" We were alone together after our rubber bridge partners had both gone home.

"Is this some sort of catch question?"

"No, but you and I both know someone who sometimes does it."

"Paddy?"

"Yes. He did it once last night in our Teams match. I have drawn two diagrams for you. This one shows his cards and the auction, so put yourself in his position (South) and see if you can deduce what he deduced. West's opening lead was the three of hearts to dummy's five and East's Jack. Perhaps he paused for half a minute, after which he made his contract with complete confidence."

East	South	West	North
1NT	NB	2♣	NB
2♦	NB	NB	Dbl
NB	2NT	NB	3NT

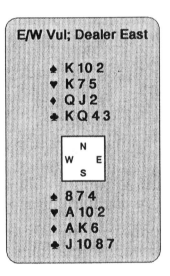

E/W Vul; Dealer East

♠ K 10 2
♥ K 7 5
♦ Q J 2
♣ K Q 4 3

♠ 8 7 4
♥ A 10 2
♦ A K 6
♣ J 10 8 7

"Let me just think a bit, he's got twenty-six points, which means that the rest, or nearly all the rest, must be in East's hand for his no-trump bid. What an extraordinary bid of Stayman by West, who can't have more than two. East has got no four-card major, so West just leaves him in two diamonds. Why didn't West pass or make a misery two-of-a-major bid? I think he must have a very bad 4-4-5-0 hand."

"Splendid. Go on. Why does West lead the three of hearts?"

"I suppose he might after all have a heart honour – let's say he has four to the Jack . . . no. East plays the Jack, try the Queen for West, leaving East with exactly twelve points."

"You did magnificently, I shall have to tell Paddy that he's not the only one to see through the backs of the cards. Now take a look at the whole hand. It's almost exactly as you described, except that West hasn't got five diamonds, which is perhaps why he bid and led as he did. Now

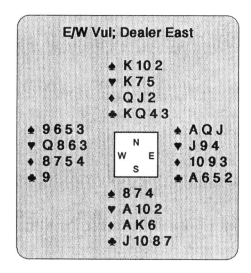

E/W Vul; Dealer East

```
                    ♠ K 10 2
                    ♥ K 7 5
                    ♦ Q J 2
                    ♣ K Q 4 3
   ♠ 9 6 5 3                      ♠ A Q J
   ♥ Q 8 6 3        N             ♥ J 9 4
   ♦ 8 7 5 4     W     E          ♦ 10 9 3
   ♣ 9             S              ♣ A 6 5 2
                    ♠ 8 7 4
                    ♥ A 10 2
                    ♦ A K 6
                    ♣ J 10 8 7
```

picture Paddy playing the hand with his usual smoothness. He ducked the Jack of hearts, won the next heart, led a club to the King and Ace, won the third round of hearts, and played off six minor-suit winners. He had won eight of the first ten tricks and had left each player with nothing but three spades! Now of course, he could duck a spade to East's Jack, lose to the Ace and win his ninth trick with the King. Nothing to it. All the thinking had gone on before."

"This was your Teams match? What happened in the other room?"

"Ah, that's the interesting thing. Our team's East and West were wiser than the young pair against us. In their case, neither of them bid. South opened one no-trump, and North raised him to three. Our West led a spade and South lost three spades, one club and one heart, going one down."

"Was it a young team, as a whole, against you?"

"Yes. Why?"

"Shall I tell you what I think? I think that what you have really been telling me, apart from how clever Paddy is, is 'Don't open one no-trump just because you've got twelve points' and 'Don't Stayman with a bad hand' and (in two words) 'grow up'!"

"Oh dear! Am I as obvious as all that?"

TAKE CARE

It was too late for another rubber, but Paddy had a suggestion to make. "Let's see," he said to me, "how our young friends would have bid that curious board last night."

He and I had managed to win the Senior Pairs competition the day before and had so far given no details to my granddaughter and young Bruce. So the cards were brought out again, and they were each given a hand and told that they were playing pairs, she being the dealer, South, and he North, both sides vulnerable and no opposition bidding.

"Which of you two actually was South?" asked my granddaughter, as she sorted her cards.

"We'll tell you later," answered Paddy. "All you need to know is that this board provided us with one of our tops."

"Right, then here goes. Two spades."

After the auction they were shown each other's cards. "How does that strike you both now?" I asked. "Are you pleased with your contract?"

"It looks as if seven is on," said Bruce. "I suppose I ought not to have bid that negative two no-trumps."

"And I think I can now guess," said my granddaughter, "what happened yesterday. You were South (I'm sure of that because Paddy wouldn't have brought up the hand if he'd been the hero) and you bid and made the grand slam."

"He was the hero all right," said Paddy, "but not quite in the way you think. Before you see the whole deal, here are some interesting facts for you. Yours indeed was the popular contract, the small slam, and it went down on *every* occasion, sometimes one down, sometimes two. The grand slam was bid twice, once at our table, but not by your grandfather, who, in fact, was *West*. Here's the whole thing with the bidding that actually occurred at our table.

Game All; Dealer South

```
        ♠ K 9
        ♥ 9 6 5 2
        ♦ A 10 7 5 3
        ♣ 8 3
              N
          W       E
              S
        ♠ A Q J 10 8 3
        ♥ —
        ♦ K 4
        ♣ A K 6 5 2
```

South	North
2♠	2NT
3♣	3♠
4♥	5♦
6♠	End

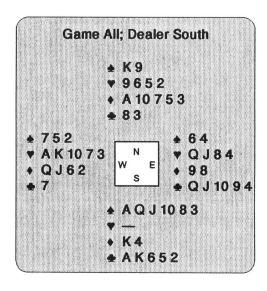

Game All; Dealer South

```
              ♠ K 9
              ♥ 9 6 5 2
              ♦ A 10 7 5 3
              ♣ 8 3

♠ 7 5 2              ♠ 6 4
♥ A K 10 7 3   N    ♥ Q J 8 4
♦ Q J 6 2    W   E  ♦ 9 8
♣ 7             S   ♣ Q J 10 9 4

              ♠ A Q J 10 8 3
              ♥ —
              ♦ K 4
              ♣ A K 6 5 2
```

South	North
1♠	1NT
3♣	3♦
3♠	4♠
5♦	6♣
7♣	End

"You can see now why there was trouble. West leads the Ace of hearts; South ruffs and sees the chance of ruffing two clubs in dummy; West ruffs the second club and of course leads a trump; South can ruff one club only and must lose two clubs and the ruff.

One or two clever declarers played a low club at the third trick, instead of the King, thus losing only two clubs in all, but no-one could make either slam."

"I don't understand what happened at *your* table," complained my granddaughter.

"Ah, we'd better ask your grandfather about that."

"All that happened," I said, "was that I did *not* lead the Ace of hearts. No sane declarer bids a grand slam without first round control of all suits. I simply did what I was taught to do sixty years ago – I led a trump against a grand slam."

"South couldn't even ruff one club, "explained Paddy, "so we had him *four* down vulnerable. The annoying thing is that only the two really spineless declarers made plus scores by not calling more than four spades."

"Thank you, Paddy. We've learnt something, haven't we, Bruce?"

"To be spineless bidders?"

"No, to take a good look at whoever is likely to make the opening lead and, if he seems rather nice but a little crafty, no grand slam!"

NEARLY THERE

"What was in your mind after the first five tricks?" I asked my granddaughter.

As often with our family rubber bridge four, the other two had gone home, and we stayed seated to discuss any hand that had interested or worried either of us. She had been greatly disappointed by the last deal of the evening, when she had failed to make a three no-trump contract and secure the rubber. We could remember the cards well enough and set them out.

South	North
1NT	2NT
3NT	End

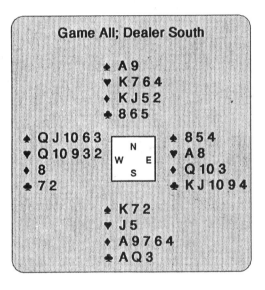

Game All; Dealer South

```
                    ♠ A 9
                    ♥ K 7 6 4
                    ♦ K J 5 2
                    ♣ 8 6 5
♠ Q J 10 6 3                      ♠ 8 5 4
♥ Q 10 9 3 2      N              ♥ A 8
♦ 8            W     E           ♦ Q 10 3
♣ 7 2             S              ♣ K J 10 9 4
                    ♠ K 7 2
                    ♥ J 5
                    ♦ A 9 7 6 4
                    ♣ A Q 3
```

I was West and had led the Queen of spades, ducked all round, then the three to dummy's Ace. At this point she crossed over to her Ace of diamonds and lost the diamond finesse to East's Queen. East (Paddy) had then led the Jack of clubs to her Queen. She had thus won three of the first five tricks.

"I asked myself," she told me now, "whether there was any better chance of a ninth trick (I could see eight) than playing and praying for the Ace of hearts to be on my left. You had shown up with that horrid singleton diamond and were likely to have more hearts than Paddy, so the odds were on your having the Ace. So I first ran my three diamond winners, then led a heart to the King and lost three heart tricks and the contract."

"I think you might have asked yourself a different question – I found myself asking it. Why had East led a club? I knew, and so did you, from the first two tricks that he held a third spade. Why didn't he continue the suit?"

"Because, of course, he knew I still had the King."

"He had a better reason than that, easy for me to spot, possible for you –

he knew I had no entry card. And he could only know that because he held the Ace of hearts and the King of clubs himself!"

"All right, then, I suppose I can put him with the Ace of hearts. So what can I do about it?"

"I'm not sure. Let's see. One thing occurs to me at once, and that is that you could safely play your King of spades at any moment. I'm trying to remember what our discards were on your diamond winners. I must have made four discards, and Paddy two, and at that point we all had five cards left. It must have been like this.

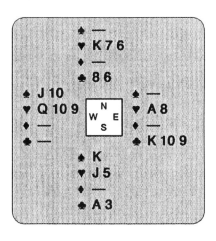

"You were on lead and needed three more tricks. You led a heart, lost three hearts and went one down. Suppose you had led the King of spades instead. Paddy probably throws the revealing nine of clubs, and now all you need to do is play Ace and another club, and he has to let you make the King of hearts and the contract."

"Suppose he throws the eight of hearts instead of a club."

"Then you lead a heart to his Ace and make the King of hearts, as before."

"So I was actually within five tricks of endplaying an expert? It's my best ever!"

NOT TO WORRY

"There are four cards of your long suit out against you," said my granddaughter, "including the Queen and the Jack, and on the first round your Ace drops the Jack. Is it true that, all things being equal, the odds are slightly in favour of your King dropping the Queen on the next round?"

North	South
1♣	1♥
4♥	4NT
5♥	6♥

"All things are never equal at the bridge table," I said cautiously.

"Oh, you know what I mean — when there's no evidence of how the cards lie. This was rubber bridge at the club I'm talking about. Four young players – all highly promising, especially me. I was South in this hand, and

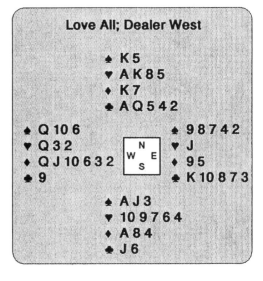

Love All; Dealer West

```
                    ♠ K 5
                    ♥ A K 8 5
                    ♦ K 7
                    ♣ A Q 5 4 2
  ♠ Q 10 6                        ♠ 9 8 7 4 2
  ♥ Q 3 2           N             ♥ J
  ♦ Q J 10 6 3 2  W   E           ♦ 9 5
  ♣ 9               S             ♣ K 10 8 7 3
                    ♠ A J 3
                    ♥ 10 9 7 6 4
                    ♦ A 8 4
                    ♣ J 6
```

West led the Queen of diamonds against my six hearts. I won in dummy and led the Ace of trumps, dropping East's Jack. Now I had to choose between playing the King and coming to hand to take a heart finesse. I tried the drop and went one down, loosing a heart and later a club."

"Did East play the nine of diamonds on the first trick?"

"Yes. What's that got to do with it?"

"You could put East with a doubleton diamond."

"Why not a singleton?"

"Because promising young players invariably open seven-card suits, no matter how weak, with three-bids, so West only had six! You could begin thinking about distribution. 'All was no longer equal', so why not explore further? What about three rounds of spades, ruffing the third?"

"I can't see what good that does."

"Nor can I for the moment. Suppose you go on by returning to hand and running the Ten of hearts. Yes, that's it. If East has the Queen, he wins but has to lead either a club into dummy's tenace or a spade, giving you a ruff and discard. But as the cards lie, the Ten of hearts wins, so you can draw the Queen."

"So it didn't really matter where the Queen was? How absurd. But the point is that later I had to play another small slam and had rather the same sort of trouble again. I dropped another early Jack. Look.

South	North
2♥	2♠
3♥	3NT
6♥	Pass

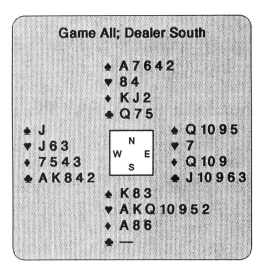

Game All; Dealer South

```
              ♠ A 7 6 4 2
              ♥ 8 4
              ♦ K J 2
              ♣ Q 7 5
♠ J                      ♠ Q 10 9 5
♥ J 6 3         N        ♥ 7
♦ 7 5 4 3    W     E     ♦ Q 10 9
♣ A K 8 4 2     S        ♣ J 10 9 6 3
              ♠ K 8 3
              ♥ A K Q 10 9 5 2
              ♦ A 8 6
              ♣ —
```

"This time there were five of the suit, spades, out against me. I ruffed West's opening Ace of clubs, drew trumps and led a small spade, on which appeared West's Jack. I won in dummy and thought that my best chance was to play for a 3-2 division of the suit, so I led another spade to my King and went down a second time, losing a spade and a diamond."

"I see. When you have to lose a trick in a suit anyhow, it sometimes pays to lose it at once. You had to lose one spade, so why not simply duck West's Jack on the first round? He can't lead a club without giving you a trick, so he tries a diamond to your Ace. Now you can play King and Ace of spades, ruff a spade, cross to dummy's King of diamonds and throw your last diamond on the established spade."

"Don't tell me that once again, it didn't matter where the Queen of spades was . . . It didn't? Then I've been worrying myself for three hours and you for three minutes over nothing at all."

"I rather enjoy it – as long as you keep it that way round!"

NOTHING SPECIAL

My granddaughter says that I am too modest when telling her about hands played at the club and never mention personal triumphs. She has a touching belief that these occur, and for once this morning I was able to remember a success of which I was proud. She likes working things out for herself, so I gave her this diagram. "I was South," I explained, "and West led the nine of spades against my four heart contract. I'm going to tell you the cards of the first four tricks, and then *you* are going to tell *me* what West and East still hold, and how I played the hand. You may also know that I got it right for a change. Are you ready?"

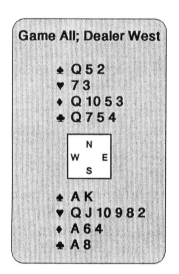

West	North	East	South
NB	NB	1♠	4♥
End			

Game All; Dealer West

♠ Q 5 2
♥ 7 3
♦ Q 10 5 3
♣ Q 7 5 4

♠ A K
♥ Q J 10 9 8 2
♦ A 6 4
♣ A 8

"Let me find a pencil, and I'm ready for anything."

"On the opening nine of spades came dummy's two, East's Ten, and my King. Next, on my Queen of hearts came the four, the three, and East's King. The third trick consisted of East's eight of spades, my Ace, West's three and dummy's five. Lastly, I led the Jack of hearts, on which West discarded the eight of diamonds, and the trick was won by East's Ace. While he pondered, I did the same. Now, please, be as brilliant as I was."

"All right. I've got the major suits pinned. West started with two small spades, East with six to the Jack; West had a singleton heart, East four to the Ace-King. That leaves East with only three minor-suit cards – and that's as far as I can get. No, wait a minute, East had only eight points in the majors. He must have one of the minor-suit kings, if not both, for his opening bid."

"Well done. Go on."

"I'm stuck. Prod me by asking a question."

"Does East's return of the eight of spades at trick three tell you anything?!

"Oh, yes, of course. East was hoping that his partner could ruff and lead back the higher of the minor suits, diamonds. But that doesn't make sense, because West discarded a high diamond. East and West can't both have the King. I've got it – East has a diamond void."

"You're nearly there. But I'm afraid that at trick five East led a diamond – the Jack."

There was silence while she began to write. "How's this then," she asked, "for the complete hand? I've guessed some of the small cards, of course."

"Absolutely right!!! I congratulate you. Now comes the easy part. I had worked it out as you did. So how do you play it?"

"You had already lost two of the first four tricks, when East led the Jack of diamonds. If you let it run, West wins and leads another to be ruffed, so you must win and draw trumps. I still can't see how you avoided losing a diamond and a club, I've exhausted my brilliance. You'll just have to tell me."

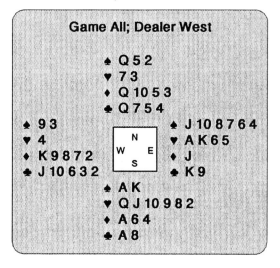

Game All; Dealer West

```
                    ♠ Q 5 2
                    ♥ 7 3
                    ♦ Q 10 5 3
                    ♣ Q 7 5 4
    ♠ 9 3                           ♠ J 10 8 7 6 4
    ♥ 4            N               ♥ A K 6 5
    ♦ K 9 8 7 2   W   E           ♦ J
    ♣ J 10 6 3 2     S             ♣ K 9
                    ♠ A K
                    ♥ Q J 10 9 8 2
                    ♦ A 6 4
                    ♣ A 8
```

"After winning with the Ace of diamonds and drawing trumps, I simply played Ace and another club, knowing that East had to win and had nothing but spades to lead. So my two black Queens in dummy became winners, on which I could throw my two losing diamonds. In that way I won four trump tricks, three spades, two clubs and one diamond . . . You look disappointed."

"No coup?"

"No coup. Coups are not really much in my line."

In spite of this, I seemed to give every satisfaction and I was duly rewarded.

WHAT'S IN A NAME?

I am finding that partnering my granddaughter in the Club Pairs is invigorating. We have not yet won anything, but came near it last night, thanks to two rather peculiar boards, on each of which my partner was successful in the unusual contract of five clubs doubled, bringing us two tops. She looks more innocent than she is and attracts not only more attention but also rather more doubling, especially from the gambling fraternity, than most declarers. This was the first of the boards, and she sat South.

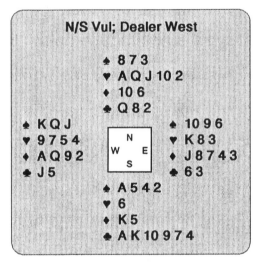

West	North	East	South
1NT	NB	NB	4♣
NB	5♣	NB	NB
Dbl	End		

N/S Vul; Dealer West

```
              ♠ 873
              ♥ A Q J 10 2
              ♦ 10 6
              ♣ Q 8 2
♠ KQJ                      ♠ 10 9 6
♥ 9 7 5 4      N           ♥ K 8 3
♦ A Q 9 2   W     E        ♦ J 8 7 4 3
♣ J 5          S           ♣ 6 3
              ♠ A 5 4 2
              ♥ 6
              ♦ K 5
              ♣ A K 10 9 7 4
```

I had as little right to put her into game as she had to make her startling jump into the auction, but this was Pairs and, once one has broken away from the room, one might as well do it properly. West led the King of spades. South won, drew trumps with Ace and King, confidently (it seemed) led her heart to dummy's Ace, ruffed out East's King of hearts, crossed to the Queen of trumps, discarded three spades on the three established hearts, and led a diamond, losing only to the Ace and Queen. She was slightly flushed but still demure and received our opponents' badinage with composure.

Later came this board. *(see next page).*

This took her a little longer, but there was only one marked pause, half-way through the second trick. She ruffed the opening King of diamonds, led a small trump and stopped to stare at West's diamond discard. Recovering, she won the trick in dummy and proceeded to ruff no fewer than four more diamonds, reentering dummy with the three major suit winners. In this way she made *eight* trump tricks in all and her contract, losing only a spade and a heart. She once again had little to say at the time, and it was not until we were on our way home that I knew how excited she had been by the two boards.

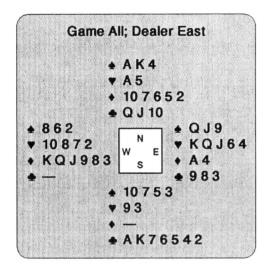

Game All; Dealer East

      ♠ A K 4
      ♥ A 5
      ♦ 10 7 6 5 2
      ♣ Q J 10

♠ 8 6 2   ♠ Q J 9
♥ 10 8 7 2   N   ♥ K Q J 6 4
♦ K Q J 9 8 3 W   E   ♦ A 4
♣ —   S   ♣ 9 8 3

      ♠ 10 7 5 3
      ♥ 9 3
      ♦ —
      ♣ A K 7 6 5 4 2

East	South	West	North
1♥	3♣	3♥	4♣
4♥	5♣	NB	NB
Dbl	End		

"Both times," she confessed to me, "I thought I could see ten tricks and had no real idea how to try for another one."

"In that first one it was brilliant play on your part not to take the heart finesse, which would have put East in to lead a diamond and send you three down."

"I was on the point of finessing the heart and suddenly thought not."

"Why? The betting was on West's having the King."

"I saw that I could never take another heart finesse. I thought that the only way of running the suit and throwing all my three little spades was to do what I did. What were our rather nice opponents joking about – something about my being backward?"

"They were congratulating you on your 'backward' (or 'ruffing') finesse."

"Is that what it's called? Then in that second board I rather lost my head, so I must have been lucky. I stopped drawing trumps when I saw West's void and simply started ruffing out anything in sight."

"Thus bringing off a sort of dummy reversal play – the longest one, I think, I've ever seen."

"Oh, that had a name too, had it? It's just as well I didn't know it at the time, I'd have been scared. I don't understand dummy reversals and I've never heard of a backward finesse!"

FAIR ENOUGH

"I'm not going to bother you after all," announced my granddaughter.

"Good. What about?"

"This – from last night's rubber bridge. I meant to ask you to settle a bet, but I've just managed to solve the problem myself."

"Is that a diagram? Let me see if I can spot the problem."

I studied the diagram. "I believe," I said slowly, "that you were North, and Bruce South; that West led the eight of spades; that South went one down; that I know why; that he blamed your second bid; that you blamed his play; that one of you (you, I fancy) made the bet; and that I was supposed to decide who won."

"You're exactly right! How do you do it?"

"At my age, you mean? It *is* rather remarkable. My only difficulty was telling which of you was which. I put you in the North seat because you are the more optimistic bidder, and the rest was easy. After the standard opening lead, the average declarer . . . do you mind, either of you, being an average declarer?"

```
                    Game All; Dealer West

                         ♠ 7 4
                         ♥ A 8 6 4
                         ♦ A K 10 2
                         ♣ A K 7
          ♠ A K J 8 5        N          ♠ 9 2
          ♥ J 9 5 3       W     E       ♥ 10 7
          ♦ Q                S           ♦ J 9 5 3
          ♣ Q 10 6                       ♣ 8 5 4 3 2
                         ♠ Q 10 6 3
                         ♥ K Q 2
                         ♦ 8 7 6 4
                         ♣ J 9
```

West	North	East	South
1♠	Dbl	NB	1NT
NB	3NT	End	

"It's a compliment."

"The average declarer wins, leads a diamond, is startled by the appearance of the Queen, wins again, sees various chances of nine tricks, cannot resist first trying another high diamond in the hope of dropping the Jack, and is disappointed."

"You're right again. Bruce next tried the hearts, and they did not break, so he turned to the clubs, playing Ace, King, and another. Unfortunately, West saw what was happening and unblocked, so the third club went to East, and that was that. *But* I've been thinking. All Bruce had to do was throw West in with the fourth heart instead of playing on clubs. Now West has to give him a spade trick or lead away from the Queen of clubs.

There's your ninth trick."

"Very neat. There is only one trouble, I think. West may not lead *away* from the Queen, he may lead the Queen itself."

"What difference does that make?"

"It blocks the suit. There is no entry to dummy now."

"Good heavens, so it does. There goes my money."

"What exactly was the bet?"

"I bet Bruce that he could have made the contract."

"Oh, I daresay you might win that all right. Suppose he doesn't play a second diamond at trick three, but tries the hearts first. East shows out, and South can count West for five spades, four hearts, and therefore four minor-suit cards – one of which is the Queen of diamonds and another, he hopes, the Queen of clubs. So he does just what you suggest – throws West in with the fourth heart. Look at the position after six tricks:

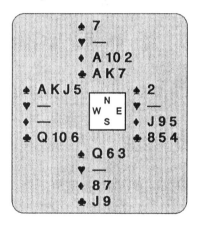

"Yes, you win your bet. West is on lead and can make two spade tricks but, no matter how he plays after that, he is bound to give South his contract. There is no longer any point in West leading the Queen of clubs, because dummy still has a diamond entry. By the way, if it turns out that after all West has the Jack of diamonds instead of a club, the minor suits break and South gets an overtrick."

"Beautiful. I'd never have spotted all that. I'm beginning to think I'll have trouble in making Bruce pay up! Perhaps I ought to call the bet off."

"Now that you've dragged me into it, why not let me decide for you?"

"I'm rather suspicious of you now – you look mischievous. All right, you decide."

"Bruce played the hand wrongly and was also wrong, in my opinion, in criticising your bid – you had every right to expect him to hold rather more than just a spade guard. On the other hand, you didn't really know how he could have made it, or even that he went wrong at trick three. We only got at it ourselves by seeing all the cards. I think you both lose. I hope the bet was a large one."

"Why, if nobody wins? Actually, it was 50p."

I found the right coin, dropped it in the R.S.P.C.A. box which was at hand, and pronounced sentence. "You both owe me 25p," I said.

ONLY HUMAN

"Would you like to solve a difficult defence problem?" I asked my granddaughter.

"Yes, please. Really difficult?"

"Too difficult for me. Paddy solved it after it was all over, but admits that he might not have done any better than I did at the table. You are East playing rubber bridge. You dealt and opened one spade, but were soon disillusioned by South's jump to five diamonds. West's opening lead is the three of spades to the Jack and your Ace, and South ruffs. He leads the King of hearts. Over to you now. You win with the Ace and lead what?"

East	South	West	North
1♠	2♦	NB	2NT
NB	5♦	End	

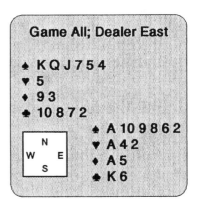

Game All; Dealer East

♠ K Q J 7 5 4
♥ 5
♦ 9 3
♣ 10 8 7 2

       ♠ A 10 9 8 6 2
       ♥ A 4 2
       ♦ A 5
       ♣ K 6

"The obvious answer, which, I suppose, must be wrong, is another spade for partner to overruff – no, that's silly, because South must hold all the trump honours and can ruff high. Why did South lead that heart? He must want to ruff a heart in dummy, and I can stop that. I lead Ace and another trump. How's that?"

"That is exactly what I did. The ridiculous thing is that we both knew the reason why it must be wrong. You have just told me it – if South holds all the top trump honours, bar the Ace, dummy's nine is a winner, and all we are doing is putting him into dummy, which is where he wants to be, and drawing trumps for him. Look. Here is the whole hand, and this is what actually happened. After winning the second trick with the Ace of hearts, I led the Ace and five of diamonds, which was allowed to run to dummy's nine. Now that I had carefully stripped my partner of his two trumps, South discarded his two losing hearts on the spade honours, took a successful club finesse and tabled his cards. I could not have chosen a worse lead. A spade, a heart or a club would have been equally ineffective, but would at least have made him stop to think about things like drawing trumps."

"But that means that there isn't a solution to your problem, and yet you say that Paddy found one."

"There is still one lead that neither of us even considered – the *five* of trumps! South lets it run to dummy's nine, of course, but now he can't make a spade trick because of West's remaining trump. He takes the club finesse, ruffs one of his losing hearts, returns to hand with a spade ruffed high, draws trumps losing to the Ace, regains the lead, but can't get rid of his second losing heart and goes down."

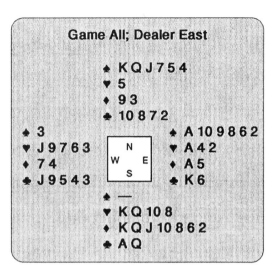

Game All; Dealer East

♠ K Q J 7 5 4
♥ 5
♦ 9 3
♣ 10 8 7 2

♠ 3
♥ J 9 7 6 3
♦ 7 4
♣ J 9 5 4 3

N
W E
S

♠ A 10 9 8 6 2
♥ A 4 2
♦ A 5
♣ K 6

♠ —
♥ K Q 10 8
♦ K Q J 10 8 6 2
♣ A Q

"How on earth can East find that lead at the third trick?"

"By putting South with seven diamonds, West with two, noting, as you did, that South wants to ruff a heart or hearts, and seeing that any other lead is almost certainly wrong, but that the five of trumps might just be right. By the way, I had one small thing to be thankful for. South might well have doubled my opening one spade, instead of calling two spades, and North would surely have left it in. I think that might have meant 800 above the line to them and still the chance of winning the rubber."

"What an extraordinary hand. I'm really quite glad that you didn't find that lead. I somehow prefer a grandfather who belongs to this world."

"While he still can, you mean?"

OTHER MR BRIDGE TITLES INCLUDE

The Bridge Player's Dictionary

The Bridge Plus Annual (The Original)

The Bridge Plus Annual (1992 Edition)

Passport to Duplicate Bridge

Bridge Plus (The magazine)   –   Edited by Elena Jeronimidis

FORTHCOMING TITLES

Teachers' Tips

Bridge Among the Penguins

The Labours of Hercules